"Every divorce sinks to the level of the most irrational party."

Melvin Belli

"Snow White doesn't marry Hitler, so no one party is ever 100% at fault."

Anonymous divorce lawyer

"Criminal lawyers see the worst people at their best. Divorce lawyers see the best people at their worst."

Thomas B. Concannon, former divorce lawyer

"It's difficult to tell which gives some couples the most happiness, the minister who marries them, or the judge who divorces them."

Mary Wilson Little, I Do to I'll Sue

"My wife got the house, the bank account, and if I marry again and have children, she gets them, too."

Woody Allen, twice divorced

"You know, if there was a nice ceremony like getting married for divorce, it'd be much better."

John Lennon

SUCCESSFUL LONE STAR DIVORCE

How to Cope
With a Family Breakup in Texas

By Ike Vanden Eykel
Managing Partner
Koons, Fuller, Vanden Eykel & Robertson

Edited By
Larry Upshaw

Published by
PSG Books
Dallas, Texas

A softcover original

Published by

Books Division
203 Lake Ridge Village, Suite 405 Dallas, Texas 75238
1-800-465-1508

SUCCESSFUL LONE STAR DIVORCE:
HOW TO COPE WITH A FAMILY BREAKUP IN TEXAS
The Texas Edition in the Successful Divorce Series
© 1998 by Professional Solutions Group

ISBN 0-9659273-1-8

Library of Congress Catalogue Card Number 98-67175

Manufactured in the United States of America

10 9 8 7 6 5 4 3 2 1

Note from the Publisher:

Most statutes pertaining to divorce and the custody of children are a matter of state law. And laws vary widely from state to state. The Successful Divorce series is comprised of published works written, edited and published according to the specifics of the laws of each state.

SUCCESSFUL LONE STAR DIVORCE: HOW TO COPE WITH A FAMILY BREAKUP IN TEXAS is the second in this series. The Alabama Edition was the first. In each case, the publisher retained the services of an accomplished family law specialist to serve as author. Some features that are common to divorce in every state may be repeated from one edition to another.

The author of this edition contributed his experience in the courtrooms of Texas and in working with clients under the laws of the state to present a well-rounded and reasonable account of how to obtain The Successful Divorce in Texas.

Achieving The Successful Divorce means that you conduct yourself in a way that allows you and your family to emerge emotionally and financially intact from the process of divorce. Everyone involved in the divorce process — the divorcing parties, their children and other family members, friends and co-workers, attorneys and those in the court system — bears some responsibility for making certain that people's lives are not ruined by this difficult and emotional event.

Accomplished family law specialists across the country who share The Successful Divorce philosophy and are interested in being the author of a statewide edition may contact PSG Books, 203 Lake Ridge Village, Suite 405, Dallas, Texas 75238, (214) 340-6223.

Notice

State laws and legal precedents vary greatly and change over time. Because of this, the reader should not use this book for specific legal advice. Every divorce case and post-divorce action is unique. It must be understood, therefore, that this book will provide readers with a general overview of the divorce process and post-divorce issues, so that they may take legal action or otherwise address these issues from a more informed position. This book is not intended to provide legal advice; you should consult an attorney for specific information related to your personal situation.

Except in a few cases where full names, places and dates are given, the people described in this book are not meant to represent anyone living or deceased. Some names or fact patterns have been invented or consolidated, to protect the privacy of the parties involved and to better illustrate an important point in the divorce process.

Any similarities between actual people or situations and the characters described in this book are, as noted above, purely coincidental.

Table of Contents

Part Five
Once Your Divorce Is Final

Introduction

Even before there was a state of Texas, there was divorce here. It all started with the Texas Divorce Act of 1841, which preceded statehood by four years. The land that we know as Texas was a vast wilderness populated by very few people. Back then, there were few grounds for dissolving a marriage. No attorneys specialized in divorce and there were no courts that handled family cases exclusively.

In fact, there were so few divorces that family issues were considered trivial matters of law. When cases did come to court, witnesses usually were not called and there were few, if any, experts in divorce and the welfare of children.

The Texas Divorce Act, an amalgam of English common law and ancient Roman custom, had a simple way of approaching property. In most cases, the man was king unless he agreed to bestow property upon his soon-to-be ex. In a prime example of the evolution of social thought, children were considered the father's property and usually stayed with him.

Throughout the 19th and early 20th centuries, as Texas remained mostly rural, divorce was an option only in the most extreme circumstances — a spouse abandoning the family, becoming mentally incapacitated or engaging in domestic violence.

During World War II, suddenly men were thousands of miles from home while their wives worked in the factories and took care of themselves and their children. At the end of the war, women welcomed their men home. They didn't, however, welcome the end of all that freedom. The number of divorces began to grow through the late 1940s, 50s and 60s, and splitting up became easier and more accepted with the adoption of no-fault statutes in the 1970s.

Increases in personal freedom during the last few decades may have been good for individual well-being, but it's played havoc on the institution of marriage, with half of all unions ending in a broken home.

The popular concept of divorce is built around a set of stereotypes depicting what happens when you leave your lover. We see divorce, inevitably, as a time for mean-spirited, nasty action. The thought is that happy lives must necessarily end at this time — that men lose their shirts, while women and their children are condemned to poverty.

Those of us who make our careers in the family courts see people destroy each other for the sake of revenge. I've seen clients — against my advice — squander every last dollar between them just to get even. I've seen them use the children as psychological battering rams against perceived or real slights and acts of omission. I've seen the most loving couples try to eviscerate each other just to see the other one bleed.

Decades of warfare can leave an attorney no longer able to see the trees or any other part of the forest. I just want to shed some light on a process that doesn't have to be so destructive.

Many people believe the answer is to make divorce more difficult to obtain. Some states are rethinking their no-fault statutes, so that married people must have a real and compelling reason for divorce. Some would make it more difficult for people to get married in the first place. But attempting to control the behavior of our citizens is a form of social engineering that is doomed to fail.

An alternative, known as The Successful Divorce, has a much greater chance to improve the lives of those people who will get a divorce, and the lives of their children. The idea behind The Successful Divorce is that your family can emerge from divorce safe and sane. People can rebuild their lives. Children do not have to be scarred for life.

All it takes is focus on the objective of The Successful Divorce, rather than on pulling your ex's heart out through an orifice and tacking it on the wall. It takes the teamwork of attorney, client, family and friends, all working toward this goal.

Now, don't get me wrong; The Successful Divorce isn't some soft approach of letting the other side push you around for the sake of keeping the peace. On the contrary, I believe in the concept of peace through strength. Sometimes you have to place your six-gun on the table, in plain sight, to forestall an attack. Just understand that you have that gun for protection, not to blow your ex's fingers and toes off, as appealing as that may sound from time to time.

The Successful Divorce is a process of "getting to yes" so that people can move on constructively.

The purpose of SUCCESSFUL LONE STAR DIVORCE: HOW TO COPE WITH A FAMILY BREAKUP IN TEXAS is to preach the gospel of the constructive life after divorce. This book is the Texas edition in The Successful Divorce series. The examples used here were taken from my experiences over two decades in the family courts, along with anecdotes and fact patterns related to me by clients, other attorneys, judges and court personnel.

Most of my time is spent in the courtrooms of Texas. But I'm also called in as a specialist in various aspects of matrimonial law in courts across the nation. The reality is that state law determines the way family court actions proceed, and those actions can be vastly different from state to state.

SUCCESSFUL LONE STAR DIVORCE is based on the statutes and

controlling case law in force in Texas at the time of publication. I
cannot be held responsible for changes in the law between the publication date and the time you read this. But when changes in an as-
pect of divorce are anticipated, I try to make you aware of that possibility in this text.

Although the special nature of Texas law applies to this entire
work, clients throughout the nation will have some common experiences in family courts. I recommend that no matter where you get a
divorce, you hire a specialist in family law. You will need to prepare
for trial. A judge or a jury, or both, will determine your fate if you
are not able to resolve your case. You have the power to control the
process yourself through settlement.

Let me also emphasize that my approach to this book is gender-
neutral. Over the years, I have represented both men and women
with equal intensity and interest. Some of my earliest successes were
in winning custody of children for fathers. At the time, this was the
cutting edge of family law litigation, and so that's where I was. But
two of my most famous cases were won for women. The Edelman
case in 1987 resulted in a book, MY HUSBAND IS TRYING TO KILL ME,
and a TV movie, *Dead Before Dawn.* In 1989, I successfully represented Josephine Cauble against her husband, Rex Cauble, a mil-
lionaire rancher, convicted drug dealer and head of the Cowboy Mafia.

I use these examples to assure you that I attempted in this book
to show no bias toward either husband or wife, or toward attorneys
of either gender. Men and women can act equally horrible during
the marriage and with a divorce pending. There are many fine men
and women attorneys. To bridge any possible gender gap, I use "he
or she" to describe attributes that could be apparent in either gender.
The only time I'm not gender-neutral is when the use of a different

wording would sound odd or result in grammatically incorrect sentences.

Many of my references to cases and clients are composites instead of being actual, individual people. One very important lesson I've learned in family law is that most divorcing people don't want the fact of their divorces advertised, and I will not violate the privacy of those who are sensitive to publicity.

Just as people are different from each other, so are the facts of each case. And the outcome of a case is dependent on the facts as well as the personalities involved. You may have a case with facts that sound much like those mentioned in one of our examples. This similarity does not ensure a similar outcome.

SUCCESSFUL LONE STAR DIVORCE should not be used as a replacement for specific legal advice. It is not a how-to book. The Successful Divorce happens when you work in tandem with a family law specialist, your friends and family to make it happen.

I would like to acknowledge the help of my staff, associates and partners, who have helped me greatly in my practice. A special thanks goes to my wife, Cathy, for her constant support through the years.

— Ike Vanden Eykel

About the Author

I remember when Ike Vanden Eykel became my lawyer. It was 1985, the year he won custody of my son for me in a Dallas Family District Court.

As the jury filed into the courtroom after a three-day trial and many hours of deliberation, I distinctly remember looking over at him. I was reminded of that famous scene from the 1960s movie *Papillon,* after Steve McQueen had spent months in the darkness of solitary confinement in a French prison.

"How do I look?" asked the McQueen character. His friend, lying to him, said he was in the pink.

Ike looked as though he'd been locked away, without sunlight or proper nourishment, for several months. He'd given me all the attorney he had. Luckily, it was enough.

Ours was an early victory for men seeking child custody in Texas. No one thought the jury would actually rule in our favor. But the combination of an extraordinary lawyer and a willing client can go a long way in these settings. Attorney and client spend a lot of time together during one of these ordeals. Life's too short to be stuck with someone you don't like.

When I first met Ike, I knew this was someone who wouldn't let me down. We meshed our personalities into a winning strategy, and we've been friends and associates ever since. When I conceived of The Successful Divorce series, the attorney I wanted to write the Texas edition was Ike Vanden Eykel.

Over the years, Ike has been variously described as "the young, urban professional," "Mr. Nice" and other sobriquets associated with someone reasonable. He's the antithesis of the shark attorney —and being a good guy has paid off for him.

Now managing partner of the Dallas-based matrimonial law firm Koons, Fuller, Vanden Eykel & Robertson, Ike was listed among America's 10 top divorce attorneys in the January 1998 issue of *Town & Country* magazine. He was also named one of Texas' best divorce lawyers in the December 1997 issue of *Texas Lawyer.*

Over the past decade, he was twice named one of the Dallas area's top six divorce attorneys by *D Magazine* in Dallas. The February 1997 issue of the magazine listed him as one of "The Best Lawyers in Dallas & Fort Worth." This same listing, based on interviews of his peers, named him among THE BEST LAWYERS IN AMERICA.

Several years ago, Ike was depicted in a book and a television movie based on one of his most famous cases.

Ike was miffed that the movie's producers used an older, somewhat portly actor to portray him. But that casting was to be understood. Ike's actions in the courtroom usually are those of a battle-hardened old pro. He is, in fact, the baby of America's best family lawyers. Still in his 40s, he is a decade younger than most of the other attorneys mentioned in the *Town & County* article.

Another truth about him: Ike isn't a native Texan. He was born in Minnesota, grew up in suburban Chicago and went to college in Iowa. But as they say, he got here as soon as he could and graduated from Baylor University School of Law in 1973. His upbringing may be low key and Midwestern, but he has developed an unusual affinity for the can-do lifestyle of rough-and-tumble Texas.

Today, Ike lives in Plano, a Dallas suburb, with his wife and three children. He has written for and lectured extensively to attorney groups over the past two decades on specifics of family law practice.

Successful Lone Star Divorce: How to Cope With a Family Breakup in Texas is his first published book.

— Larry Upshaw
Series Editor

Will This Marriage Never End?

Alain and Cheryl Doucet filed for divorce in 1992. But six years passed before they could actually live apart.

The first three years were spent fighting about the divorce, with Cheryl wanting the house and custody of their two children, and Alain staying in their home so he didn't lose daily contact with his kids. In 1995, the judge in the case ordered both parents to remain in the home until the youngest child was 18 years old or graduated from high school.

What followed were three years their son described as "weird and divided." There were separate phone lines and televisions, as well as separate refrigerator shelves for his food and hers.

The Doucets tried to avoid each other, each of them staying away for long periods of time. But conflicts were inevitable, until the summer their son turned 18.

Alain had tired of the arrangement the previous May and moved out to get remarried. Cheryl tried to have him held in contempt of court.

"I didn't care that he was getting married," she said, "but he was breaking a court order." The judge, who refused to comment about the case, finally would not prevent the breakup.

From Associated Press reports

Part One

The Big Decision

CHAPTER ONE

Is Divorce the Answer?

Paula glared across the living room at her husband, Robert, as he stared off in space. The couple had just wound down from their umpteenth argument in 12 years of marriage. Both were flushed from the battle. The frustration left an awful, sickening feeling. It always did, whether they were fighting about money or the kids — or what color to paint the new gameroom.

At times like these, Paula wanted to run away from her pricey North Dallas neighborhood. Leave him, this house, their life. Take the kids and go, chuck it all and not look back. And for Robert, there was an ambivalence. Maybe he wanted to see her go.

Divorce: Easy Way Out
Or The Only Way to Go?

For at least half the couples facing this scenario, divorce has been the preferred path over the last several decades. As everybody knows, Texas is a big state. It's also a big state for divorce. The latest ranking places Texas 13th among all the states with 5.3 divorces per thousand people, 20 percent greater than the national average. Only Florida, among the 10 most populous states, has more divorces per capita.[1] Each day in Texas, there are 486 marriages. On that same day, 265 divorces are finalized. [2]

I have no documented proof of why divorce is so prevalent in this state. I do know that plenty of really foolish decisions have been made in the heat of passion, by people who essentially love and care for each other, but who don't think quickly enough to hold back and edit what they say or do before it becomes a harsh reality in their lives.

I practice law in the Dallas/Fort Worth Metroplex, one of the nation's largest metropolitan areas. It's a place with all the pressures and temptations known to man or woman. Most of my clients are economically advantaged, highly educated individuals from the best-known families in the area. The truth is that divorce affects every socioeconomic class and ethnic group.

That's because no matter what your pedigree, we all live in an era of throwaway relationships. Everywhere we look, people are more alienated from each other, be it kids from parents, brothers from sisters — but especially married people from one another.

Staying married is one of life's great difficulties. But history shows that getting divorced is no walk in the park.

Look at the Downside (As Well As the Upside)

You can bet that Paula and Robert, our couple at the beginning of this chapter, are looking at divorce as the answer to all their problems. In most cases, divorce creates a whole new set of problems. Divorce has taken a devastating toll on our families. Divorcing couples become more bitter and alienated. Their kids lose self-esteem and may never recover. The ripple effect of divorce can be seen in statistics on teenage crime, pregnancy, school problems and life-long psychological difficulties.

No matter how well-intentioned you are, it's impossible to escape many of these troubles if you make that fateful decision. And so, because of the detrimental effects of divorce, I tell my clients to thoroughly consider how their lives will be changed if they decide to divorce.

Take a breath, step back and see yourself as single, just for a moment. Most families can just barely pay for one household using the resources of two people. When you consider using those incomes to run two households, you can see the financial pressure you create. Those pressures are multiplied when you have children. You may be surprised how difficult it is to raise children in two separate homes. Daily responsibilities are greatly magnified with only one person doing them. You may have total responsibility for thousands of lunches, carpools, practice sessions or sporting events. You make last-minute decisions when your child is sick and you have to go to work. And you may constantly worry about the lack of good parental influences. Even though the helpfulness of another parent may be missing, that other person usually is still in the picture, not to mention that person's new mate. You may have considerable contact with your former spouse and his or her family, and that can be a source of great discomfort in itself.

At a time like this, you should consider the use of every resource — marital or individual therapy, substance abuse counseling, the words of a pastor or the guidance of a wise friend or family member — that might help you find a way to keep your marriage together.

A friend of mine once told me that as a divorce lawyer, I could afford to talk about avoiding divorce. He said I was much like the electric utility company, which tries to give you a myriad of ways to use power efficiently, knowing that people will always use lots of electricity. He's right, in a sense, for there will always be divorce. Nevertheless, after 25 years in the divorce business, I would take a world where there was no divorce and I would practice some other kind of law.

Inform Yourself
About Property and Custody

When you move from even the worst marriage to divorce, your life is turned upside down. Everything is different. Friends and family members look at you differently. You shop for groceries with different priorities in mind. And if you have children, use of your time and energy are completely different.

The thought can be overwhelming, so I try to simplify things for my clients by telling them that only two things will really change — access to property and children.

I have a client who was married four times and has divorced three times. He has settled in with his fourth wife and says this is for life. He told me that he was tired of building up his net worth only to cut it in half, over and over again. Although being married was no easier now than when he was young, he'd miss his children too much if he left. It's not the most romantic reason to stay married, but it may be one of the most common.

The truth is, in most cases you will have less property after a divorce. And your relationship with your children will forever be changed.

Consider Your Options

I've seen plenty of marriages that could have been saved if one party or the other, usually both, made small alterations in the way they did things. If your problem is a messy house, perhaps you could find a way to afford a maid once a week. It's certainly cheaper than getting a divorce, and a lot less disruptive. So you fight over the religious upbringing of your children. Maybe there's room for some compromise, with an eye on practicing the charity that most religions espouse.

Of course, there are the "marriages from hell," with men and women who verbally, physically or even sexually abuse their mates and their children. There are spouses who spend every dollar in the household for alcohol or drugs, or to curry favor with extramarital partners. You may not want a divorce at all, but your mate could be dead set on it.

In those cases, you may have little control over whether you get a divorce.

Basic Truths of a Lone Star Divorce

I'm constantly surprised, even by people who've been divorced two or three times, how little the average person knows about divorce in Texas.

A Lone Star Divorce has it's own peculiarities. You can watch the Oprah Winfrey Show or Sally Jessy Raphael for information about how to proceed. Keep in mind that those are national shows, and they may be describing a divorce that takes place in Florida or California. Divorce is a matter of state law, for the most part, and state laws differ in how they treat certain evidence and what is under the discretion of the judge in the case.

We're talking about Texas. It's your marriage and divorce with your own particular life story. These certain things will happen, without fail, in every Texas divorce.

Truth #1: Either party in a Texas divorce, unlike in many other states, can ask for and receive a jury trial (although jury decisions that are binding on the court are limited);

Truth #2: There will be a 60-day waiting period from the time you file the divorce until it can be final, even with an uncontested divorce;

Truth #3: Your property will be divided in a manner that the judge deems "just and right" and the judge may look at future earning capacity, who's at fault for the divorce and other criteria in making a disproportionate division;

Truth #4: Unless you have no significant assets or means to support yourself or you and your spouse agree to it, there will be no significant long-term alimony once the divorce is final;

Truth #5: The spouse who does not have primary custody of the children will, in most cases, pay child support to the primary custodial parent after a divorce based on guidelines in the Texas Family Code, according to income;

Truth #6: Joint custody is preferred in this state and you will have to consider jointly parenting with your ex. Joint custody means the sharing of parental rights and duties and does not necessarily mean equal periods of possession;

Truth #7: Both parents will have significant access to their children after a divorce, if they have been involved parents during the marriage;

Truth #8: Once a divorce is filed in Texas and one party wants to go through with it, you can't stop if from happening.

These are the basic elements of a Lone Star Divorce.

CHAPTER TWO

The Decision is Made

Genna always thought that if she made a really big decision, like getting a divorce, it would be like a bolt out of the blue.

But the truth was that the decision to end her marriage was a long, painful journey. It began in college. Steve was a charming rogue. She knew about his wandering ways from the start. She saw how he looked at other women even before they were married. But she believed time and the responsibility of a family would cause him to settle down. It was after the birth of their second child and Steve's promotion to partner in the Houston office of a national commercial real estate firm that she began to feel the distance growing between them.

There were signs along the way that divorce was imminent. She would deny that because she had a family to protect. Still, there were signs that told her she had to move forward.

Cellular bills came to the house with hundreds of calls to one unfamiliar number. Credit card bills contained charges that baffled her. Then on Valentine's Day, a bouquet of roses arrived at her home.

The card was signed by her husband, but apparently the erotic message on the card was intended for someone else. The florist had mixed up the packages to his "two girls."

The next morning, Genna arrived in her lawyer's office, ready to file for divorce.

Your Spouse's Evil Twin

Rarely is divorce the perfect fix for all the problems you encounter in marriage. In fact, divorce usually comes with its own set of headaches and heart pangs. And if you've been the so-called "passive" partner in the marriage, you may be shocked at how the more active partner reacts to the divorce filing.

As you begin this process, you may not believe that the former breadwinner of your family would fight paying child support or decide to engage you in a battle for custody of your children. You may shake your head at the tenaciousness of your loving, soon-to-be ex-spouse refusing to budge an inch on negotiations that would dispose of the case and move you all to a better psychological place.

More than one client has described the situation this way: it's as though a relatively reasonable person stepped through the door and out of the marriage, and in walked that person's evil twin, ready to make a mess of the divorce.

Many of the cases I handle involve divorcing parties who come to me after settlement negotiations have broken down. In most cases, I can get talks back on track and eventually reach a settlement. But the only way that can be done is to load up, get ready for battle and march in with both guns cocked and ready.

The effect of this active armament can be shocking to people who are not accustomed to confrontation. But human nature dictates that people settle only when they determine that entering the war zone can be hazardous to their health.

From situations like this arise stories in which both parties claim to have been taken to the cleaners in the divorce.

Like the man who refused to allow his wife of more than two decades to have even her clothes, since they were in what he considered his house. It didn't matter that they both worked and paid for the house together, or that the wife's name was on the deed. In a case like this, you can only hope there's an attorney on the other side who knows family law and will explain to the client what is reasonable. Otherwise, settlement is nearly impossible. Both parties come out of the battle with deep scars. The woman in this case was dismayed that she had to fight so hard for what rightfully should have been hers. And no matter how much punishment the man inflicted on his former mate, in the end he was convinced she had come away from the marriage with too much.

Empowering Yourself

Few things lead more directly to The Successful Divorce than making a grand, sweeping decision. Settling things once and for all. Stopping all the discussion and filing for divorce.

For most people, making that decision is scary but liberating. You've thought about the downside. You know money will be tight. Taking care of children will be made more difficult. And having to see the former spouse, perhaps for decades, will not be fun.

But by making the decision, you're taking your fate into your own hands, and that is empowering.

The Company of Good Friends

A perfectly normal question people ask themselves when they first decide to divorce is this: "What will people think of me?"

You've heard all the stereotypical tales of divorce; that women always get more than 50 percent of the assets or men never get custody of the children. These things may or may not happen in your case, depending on the facts. Equally as undetermined is this question: who will get custody of the family friends?

Some friends may shun you while others rant about your soon-to-be ex. A long line of co-workers, friends and family members will offer you advice. But none of these sources knows all the secrets of your married life, and no one can give you accurate advice without all the facts.

If I did antitrust work, my clients would have few people telling them what they should or should not be doing. Everyone who walks into my office has a "cousin Vinny" who represented another cousin in divorce court in New Jersey and this is what he got. The first time I consult with them is like placing a street light in a dark alley.

In most cases, "war stories" about divorce skew your idea of what to expect and how your future life will be. Inevitably, they can damage your pursuit of The Successful Divorce.

The time to seek help from family and friends is before you decide on a divorce. Many people — embarrassed and ashamed — are reluctant to seek advice for marital problems. Your best friends will listen very calmly and simply try to be there for you. The only reason to hold back at this time is because you just aren't sure about the motives of certain friends. Remember, friends and family members often are brought into court to testify, especially when the custody of children is involved. Be very selective with the people you choose to tell your deepest secrets. Lean on family and friends for emotional support, but turn to an expert for legal advice.

Telling Your Family

Family members should rally to your defense at a significant moment like this. They should, but they don't always. Be prepared for skeptical looks and probing questions. Clients sometimes get this kind of treatment when they drop the big one.

"Why on earth would you divorce him (or her)? You'll never marry that well again."

Little did the person asking this question know that he snorted half the cocaine in North America before beating her and the kids. Or that she put the family deep in debt to finance a three-week shopping trip to New York City.

Your family may totally agree with your actions, but you should be prepared for something less. If the blessing of your family members is important to you, be ready to lay out the facts of the case in excruciating detail.

Telling Your Children

If you think friends and family members will question your motives, just wait until you talk to the children. No, don't wait. Do it as soon as you can, before they learn the bad news from someone else, or they overhear you telling someone about it on the telephone.

Shooting the messenger for bringing bad news is common. The person who tells the children about the divorce is often blamed for the breakup. Telling the children as a couple usually is the best approach, if you can put aside your antagonisms for the benefit of your kids.

I know of a woman whose scoundrel husband stayed drunk and away from home for weeks at a time. He refused to work, while she brought in an income and took care of their three children. The last straw for this woman was when she found out that her husband raided their teenage daughter's college fund to pay for his girlfriend's breast enlargement operation. If anyone deserved to bad mouth that sorry, no good you-know-what, it was this man's wife and the mother of his children. But she resisted the temptation to destroy him in the eyes of his kids. Instead, she extracted a promise that if she would restrain herself, he would return the money. And together, they told the kids about the pending divorce. It wasn't easy, but at least they came out better than if she had declared war.

Of course, your soon-to-be ex may lapse into volunteering information to the kids about what a scoundrel he is. There's little you can do about that. The truth is, the children know more than you realize. They will come to know and understand even more during the pendency of the divorce.

Telling Too Many People

There is a critical point at the beginning of most divorces when one party or the other has talked to too many people. With many people, there is a need to talk and it is very therapeutic. Remember, your words may be played back later and, most often, they get distorted by the other side.

Plenty of divorces start amicably enough. Everyone wants to

be reasonable. People are thinking only of the children. But as the word filters out to friends and family members, bits of information about the other spouse make their way back to Divorce Central.

It can be actual facts or it might just be opinions, like "I never liked him anyway." People who don't know anything about the facts of your marriage can say awful things. And then, when you've had enough, the lid blows and a divorce that might have been settled easily becomes a desperate struggle.

I recommend that anyone getting divorced sit down and make a list of friends and family who must be told or who will find out through intermediaries. Decide upfront just how much to tell each person and determine how much you want them to tell you.

Remember that in this early stage, many couples reconcile. There's nothing more embarrassing than criticizing your spouse to someone you know well, then having to take it all back if you call off the divorce. When in doubt, keep your anger to yourself for the time being.

CHAPTER THREE

Hire All the Family Lawyer You Can Afford

When Marie and Tony decided to get divorced, they agreed to keep it simple, inexpensive and civil. They sat down together and decided how to divide their property. They also agreed that their young daughter would live with Marie. Tony, an older man who was more worldly than his wife, said he didn't want the responsibility of a youngster.

After the couple made their agreements, Tony submitted it all to the same attorney he used to handle business disputes involving his San Antonio trucking company.

Marie had moved out of their home and into an apartment. With things being handled so cordially between them, Marie left her daughter in the house with Tony and they agreed to move her at the end of the school semester.

When all of the papers were drawn up, Tony came back for Marie to sign them.

"There's only one problem," he told her. "You know I don't want custody. But you haven't been in your apartment long enough, so the attorney says the judge will want the papers to say that I get custody. It's just a formality."

Marie didn't have counsel. The only lawyer she knew was a former neighbor who practiced some other kind of law, something that had to do with real estate or insurance. Tony assured her that his lawyer was acting as counsel for both of them. She signed the divorce agreement, genuinely believing that she was going to get custody of their child in spite of what the papers said, because Tony said she would.

Within a few days, Marie noticed that when she called to talk to her daughter, Tony's mood had changed. The daughter told her that Tony's secretary had moved into the bedroom she and Tony had shared.

And when Marie asked her former husband when her daughter was coming to live with her, he informed her that "the papers say I get custody," hanging up the phone and shutting their daughter out of her life.

Don't Trust Too Much

I was honored to be chosen one of America's 10 top divorce lawyers by *Town & Country* magazine. The magazine's divorce guide noted that many of my clients come to me after their cases go to hell in a hand basket. [3]

Most of the disarray I'm brought in to tidy up is caused by people trusting too much. People today get accused of being too cynical. But in matters of love, I've found that's not true. Most of the problems of divorcing people that I've encountered seem to come from misplaced trust.

Following the best pathway to The Successful Divorce seems to involve walking a fine line. You may not want to be aggressive, but you certainly want to be assertive.

Imagine for a moment what the perfect result of your divorce would be. If that picture involves your ex dangling over the Brazos River from a meat hook, perhaps you should change the scene. But a dose of realism along with your imagination is no crime.

Perhaps you see yourself in a nice home, with your children in good spirits around you, your financial condition bordering on leisurely. Then you think, how do I ensure that this is my future, not just leaving it to chance?

In the case of Marie and Tony, eventually things were straightened out. Marie got custody of her daughter, but she had to incur a tremendous financial and emotional expense to go back to court and prove that she was deceived and that the original divorce agreement was obtained through fraud. It was a hard lesson for Marie, learning not to trust someone who had been so valuable in her life.

Match Your Attorney to Your Circumstances

Here in a free country, no one puts a gun to your head and forces you to retain an attorney who charges a high hourly rate for those difficult situations. Certainly, those of us who are successful at what we do expect to be paid for our time. The chore for you is to become a smart consumer of legal services and choose the attorney who can meet your expectations at a price you can afford.

You can hire an attorney at a variety of levels. As the level rises, so do the charges. A young attorney who handles many different kinds of cases, from family law to criminal to real estate, might ask for a retainer of $1,500. From that he will subtract his time at $100 to $150 per hour.

A more experienced attorney who spends most of his time on divorce work might expect a retainer of $2,500 to $10,000 and charge $150 to $300 per hour for his time. Most attorneys at this level are board certified in family law by the Texas Board of Legal Specialization, an arm of the State Bar of Texas.

A handful of Texas attorneys who are considered the best in the nation at their specialty charge a retainer of $25,000 or more and bill for their time at an hourly rate of $400 to $500.

Why would you pay that much money to get divorced? Usually it's a matter of economics. If there is little property to divide and no children to fight over, a less experienced attorney will do nicely. You don't need a nuclear missile to destroy an ant hill.

But a partner of mine often says that "divorce is the biggest business deal most people will ever be involved in." If you own a nice home, several cars, some investments, a retirement account or two, some large insurance policies and maybe some interest in a family business, you may be surprised at your net worth.

I've sat across the desk from many seemingly middle-class people who were stunned to find several million dollars at stake in their divorce. Part of achieving The Successful Divorce is making certain you know what valuable assets are in your estate and that you retain your fair share of those assets.

Interviewing Lawyers

So what qualities does your divorce attorney need in order to do well? Some attorneys are very good at tracing assets that your soon-to-be ex may have hidden. Others may be good at fending off trouble from the other side, with an eye on keeping them off-balance. A few are excellent at obtaining custody of children.

Whatever your need, there is an attorney who can help you with it. There are more than one million attorneys in the United States. Approximately 70,000 are licensed in Texas alone. [4]

One of the best ways to locate the correct attorney for you is to ask divorced people whom they would recommend. You may know an attorney who practices in a field other than matrimonial law. Ask that attorney to refer you to a family lawyer. Your local bar association may have a referral service categorizing attorneys by specialty. Marriage counselors, accountants, financial planners, business managers and clergy often know family lawyers with outstanding reputations and good track records.

Once you have the names of several family lawyers, you should call and schedule initial interviews with them. It's important to ask upfront if the attorney charges for this first interview. There is no hard and fast rule on this.

In the initial interview, each attorney will want to cover the basic history of the marriage and the issues involved in the divorce. You should be as candid as possible, letting the attorney know all your good points and all your faults. Lawyers are under an ethical obligation not to disclose to anyone the information you provide to them, unless you consent to the disclosure. Don't worry about the shock value of what you disclose. If he or she is an experienced family lawyer, adultery, physical abuse, substance abuse or kinky sexual practices are issues he or she has heard about before.

In this first visit, a lawyer will try to distill the basic issues that are likely to be contested in the case and summarize the major assets and liabilities of the divorcing parties. You can move this process along by providing a detailed list of debts and assets and a narrative giving your history, as well as your reasons for the divorce, at the time of your first meeting.

Has Any Attorney Ever Lost a Case?

I've had clients who interviewed several attorneys tell me that, from their investigation, they assume no family lawyer has ever lost a case. Most attorneys gladly trumpet their successes, and few tell you about their failures. In actuality, only two types of attorneys have never lost a case; those who have never tried any cases and liars. To achieve The Successful Divorce, you don't want either.

At the interview stage, clients must ask the right questions. Educating yourself is at least half the benefit of this process. You'll want a rundown of the types of family law cases the attorney has handled, and the results. If you have a family business at stake, you'll want to know the attorney's experience handling complex property arrangements and the resources (accountants, business-related expert witnesses) available to provide evidence. Don't allow an attorney to generalize about past accomplishments. Demand specific information, such as the facts of the case, money amounts involved and the disposition of each case. And if you doubt the attorney's veracity, either ask for clients you can call or just move on to the next attorney on your list.

If you anticipate a fight for custody of children, ask to speak with clients who will tell you how this attorney performed in such a suit.

Most important of all, you are trying to determine if the chemistry is there between attorney and client. It is a situation of seeing if the hand fits the glove. This is a person who will know every good and bad thing about you before the divorce is final. More than in any other legal specialty, the family lawyer must be someone you don't mind spending a great deal of time with.

You may begin your attorney search wanting to hire "the meanest junk yard dog" in captivity. But meanness breeds anger, and anger results in obstructionism. A case that drags out unnecessarily costs money and in the long run may not lead you to The Successful Divorce. Some cases demand a tough-guy strategy to match the tenaciousness of the other side. What you want to find is an attorney who can use meanness as a weapon to help you, or not use it at all. You may decide that an attorney who can successfully settle a case is more to your liking.

At the end of the initial meeting, both you and the attorney will determine whether to proceed further. If so, the lawyer usually will give you some homework — a listing of additional information that will be needed to prepare the case. Also, you will be asked to execute an agreement covering legal fees and expenses.

Keeping Fees Reasonable

Have you ever hired a craftsman — a plumber or a bricklayer — and paid that person on an hourly basis? If you ask that craftsman for additional services during the course of the job, and you don't secure an estimate of additional charges, you may be shocked when the job is complete and the bill is placed before you.

The same thing applies with an attorney, only this craftsman isn't right in front of you when much of the work is being done, so that you can calculate the hours. Sometimes an attorney brings in other experts or professionals you are required to pay, even though you don't see much of their work product.

Most matrimonial lawyers charge on an hourly basis for services provided by the attorney and staff members. The clock is ticking and money is being spent each time you meet with the lawyer, he works on your case, his staff works on your case or you speak with anyone from the law office on the telephone.

For that reason, clients who use an attorney as a sounding board for all the "he said, she said" minutiae that is common in a divorce find themselves with a huge bill to pay.

Gossip, whining and endless talk will cost you money. A smarter move is to write down questions to ask and facts you want your attorney to know. You may believe a face-to-face meeting is necessary. But many items can be covered by telephone, with the attorney or the legal assistant assigned to your case.

Matrimonial law experts often return phone calls late at night or from their homes, due to court schedules. Clients sometimes try to call then, too, just to vent their complaints. This is valuable family time for many attorneys. As such, it can be expensive.

Clients know that they can reach me through my staff, at night or on the weekends, but only in emergencies that must be addressed immediately. It's important to define what your attorney considers an emergency and how much he or she charges for that time.

The combativeness of the opposing party can greatly affect the cost of your divorce. I like to determine very early in a case how much fight is in the other side. If your spouse wants his or her "day in court" when the issues involved are simple and should be settled easily, you may be in for a lengthy and expensive battle. This type of opposition often will fight everything your attorney attempts to do, resulting in significantly higher legal bills for both sides.

Initial Retainer Must Be Refundable

A saying that's been popular with family lawyers in Texas for several decades proclaims, "Gunfighters don't charge by the bullet." This means that the only real measure of an attorney's effectiveness is results, not time spent on a case. Some family attorneys have used this type of thinking to justify large nonrefundable retainers.

Most family lawyers require a retainer, which is a down payment that ensures the lawyer will be paid for the time spent and expenses incurred. Retainers ranging from $2,500 to $10,000 are common throughout Texas, although very complex cases involving large estates, complicated financial issues or difficult child custody disputes may require a retainer of $25,000 or more.

For decades, attorneys handling large divorce cases did not refund retainer money if the case settled or the client decided to hire another lawyer. Some of the more macho attorneys justified this by proclaiming that the case settled because the other side found out who the attorney was and got frightened away.

Today, though, people are wiser consumers of legal services. Few attorneys can get by without a refund policy and don't attempt to do so. Most firms requires a retainer at the start of a case. This retainer must be replenished regularly, especially just before going to trial. A contested trial may take several days or even weeks of trial time and many weeks of preparation. An attorney's fees and expenses can be considerable in a contested matter.

If a client is unwilling to pay the lawyer in the midst of a crisis, it's unlikely that the client will pay once the problem is solved. And if the attorney doesn't solve the problem to the client's complete satisfaction, collecting for the time spent can be difficult.

Dispensing advice in a divorce matter without a retainer in place is risky for the attorney. When I was younger and began to practice family law, people would call my office and say, "I don't have the money to hire you, but can I ask you some questions about my case?" This is similar to a person without money (or insurance) who finds a growth on his neck. The person calls and asks if the surgeon can say over the phone if the growth is cancer and how the patient can remove the growth himself. Neither the doctor nor the attorney can properly advise a do-it-yourselfer about these serious situations over the telephone, with any degree of effectiveness.

Your best move is somehow to find the money to hire an attorney. You may negotiate a payout or arrange a bank loan secured by something of value. Advances on credit cards or loans from a friend or relative are also possibilities. Even a client of some wealth may lack access to retainer money. A good attorney will work with you to help you find a way to secure sufficient funding for legal services.

Your Spouse May Not Pay Your Fees

One payment alternative attorneys rarely depend on anymore is the notion that a husband will be ordered to pay his wife's attorney fees at the end of a divorce. In past times, courts did order such payments in some instances. This practice is used less often as the court system has been pushed to become more gender-neutral.

You truly get what you pay for in life. If you hire a professional, you are best served to pay that person. There is danger inherent in allowing an attorney to defer payment of fees until the case is ended. This may result in the lawyer not getting paid for a long time. In such cases, you might hear an attorney use that fact as an excuse for shoddy work. You must be very clear at the outset of your divorce that you are paying for only the finest professional services.

Make Sure You Receive Regular Bills

You should insist that the attorney provide you with regular billing statements showing the time invested in your case, the expenses incurred and the balance of any retainer. Such bills should be sent to you at least once a month.

The worst situation is to spend thousands in legal fees to fight for hundreds in assets. If your spouse is being difficult, your attorney will invest many hours in the case, with fees rising accordingly. You will be obligated to pay for work done on the case, regardless of the outcome.

Preparing a case for trial may require the lawyer and staff to work many hours examining countless documents and preparing witnesses for trial. Since you have no control over the court's docket, you may not be able to determine if your case will go to trial at a particular time. Because of this fact, your attorney may come to court fully prepared for trial, only to have to come back in a few weeks after preparing all over again.

Sometimes clients are quick to say they want their lawyer to do "whatever it takes." That is the same thing as saying, "I don't care how much it costs." How often in your life have you told someone that?

These instructions can cost an incredible amount of money.

Giving your attorney this much freedom to spend your money rarely results in The Successful Divorce. This type of client often compares the value of the settlement to the amount of legal bills without considering the range of services performed by the lawyer. Monthly statements with details of services rendered are the best protection from abuse of your wallet.

Who Pays Expenses?

Most attorneys bill you separately for expenses incurred in the case, including filing fees, deposition costs and the cost of expert witnesses.

The average filing fee for a divorce action in Texas is more than $100. An important part of the discovery process, which precedes a trial, are depositions of the opposing party and some important witnesses. Deposition costs generally are based on the length of the deposition. A court reporter usually is present to record the testimony, a service that can cost several hundred dollars. You also pay for attorney's time associated with preparing for and taking the deposition.

Expert witnesses are necessary in many complex cases. If you have a family business, an accountant or business consultant may be employed to help determine the value of the business. In a contested custody trial, psychologists and psychiatrists are asked to recommend what they believe is in the best interest of the child.

Fees must be charged for serving the opposing party with pleadings, subpoenas and other related documents. If time is of the essence, a special process server can serve documents immediately, while the local sheriff's department sometimes takes several weeks. The fee for service of documents by a process server generally runs from $50 to $100 or more, depending on how difficult it is to locate and serve the individual. Many law firms charge for copies and faxes as well as other costs associated with preparing the case.

Always familiarize yourself with the anticipated costs to avoid confusion. A good attorney will have no trouble explaining costs to you.

Form a Partnership with Your Attorney

Once you choose an attorney, you have formed a short-term relationship, a partnership of sorts. You should find out what your attorney plans to do next, when you can expect the divorce to be filed and when your spouse will be served with papers. You should be made aware of developments in the case, should your spouse retaliate in response to the divorce action and the service of papers. Your attorney should be able to advise what you should do in every instance. If he or she has trouble doing that, a communications problem may become evident between the two of you that you should address immediately.

You should expect your attorney to be very specific about the procedures, time deadlines and costs involved in the process. Female clients should never tolerate an attorney saying something like, "Now, little lady, go home and don't worry your pretty little head about this. I'll take care of it."

You are the boss. Your attorney works for you, and the two of you must work together.

One thing your attorney will do is give you "homework assignments." A good attorney will make certain to know everything possible about the marriage, the reasons for the divorce and the overall history of the relationship. A narrative from you can be extremely helpful to the lawyer and the staff in preparing your case. It should be as detailed as possible. Be careful to prepare this information at work or keep it in a safe place where your spouse cannot find it. A detailed history of your ongoing adulterous relationship or a life-long homosexual affair is not something you would want to share with your soon-to-be ex.

In addition, your lawyer will need a listing of assets and debts with as much detail as you can provide. If custody is an issue, you will need to supply extensive information about your children and the parenting history of you and your spouse.

All of this is essential background information that I ask from clients in the form of written assignments. I need a time line of events, along with a witness list. This gives me more than just the information I need to formulate my case. It immerses clients in their cases and makes them think about events that have a major impact on their lives.

CHAPTER FOUR

Uncontested Divorce or Nuclear War

Maxine assumed the divorce would not be contested. She knew exactly what property she wanted from the marriage. It didn't matter what her husband, Gregory, wanted. He had always been the passive one in the relationship. There was no reason to believe the divorce would be any different.

So when Maxine went to see her lawyer, she wanted to know the fee for an uncontested divorce. "All we need is a lawyer to prepare the papers," she said.

A truly uncontested divorce is the rarest of commodities. It means that people who agree on very little in a marriage — to the point of pulling the plug on the whole thing — will come together and agree on everything involved in saying goodbye.

In the case of Maxine and Gregory, like many others, the divorce started out cordially enough. Then Gregory talked to his buddies. The next thing you knew, he was speaking up like never before. Ego, pride, jealousy, rage and resentment intermingled with substantive issues of custody and property. Someone said something that shouldn't have been said, and that earlier spirit of agreement went the way of the dodo bird. An uncontested divorce had suddenly become both contested and expensive.

How Wide the War

If you want to keep the conflict to a small skirmish, the best idea is to restrain yourself and keep your mouth shut. Many agreements that are perfectly fair to both parties wind up back in play after one spouse says something awful to the other before the papers are executed. There are good reasons to nullify agreements, but pride and ego are not among them.

Some people feel that having one attorney represent both parties is civil and smart. It may be civil, but it's not smart — and it's not ethical in most cases. You have to remember that an attorney can represent only one party in a divorce. The attorney is looking out for the best interests of one client, and the other party's rights could be greatly affected by the terms of any settlement agreement entered into between the parties.

If your spouse insists on having just one attorney, make sure it is your attorney and that the attorney is representing you. Without that kind of protection, prepare yourself for a potential disaster that could affect you the rest of your life.

Filing the Correct Documents

Even in the case of an uncontested divorce, certain documents must be prepared and presented to the court in order to assure the judge that the parties know the substance of their agreement. The party filing for divorce is the petitioner, and the opposing party is the respondent. If the divorce becomes contested at any time, many other documents can be necessary. But the basic documents the parties must file with the court include:

Petition

When people say that they've "filed for divorce," this is the document they file. It contains certain factual information about the parties, as well as the grounds for the divorce. In Texas, which has a no-fault statute, the reason for the divorce usually is incompatibility. This means the parties have different interests and have grown apart, and this condition is irreconcilable. Other grounds include mental cruelty and adultery. The petition is filed by the petitioner and served on the respondent.

Answer

This document, which generally must be filed within 20 days of the petition, is the respondent's answer to the petitioner's pleading.

Inventory

This is a detailed listing of a client's assets and liabilities. It is sworn to by the client and filed with the court.

Decree of Divorce

This document, executed by the trial judge, grants the divorce, approves any settlement agreement between the parties and makes it binding on the parties. It also may contain the full agreement of the parties, dispensing with the need for a separate document referred to as an agreement incident to divorce.

Once the necessary documents have been executed by the parties, they are filed with the court and the judge finishes the process by executing the decree of divorce. The waiting period between filing the petition and the divorce being granted is a minimum of 60 days. The reason for this waiting period is to make certain the parties have not moved too quickly. The court wants to give the parties ample time for reconciliation. If all the documents have been prepared properly and there is an agreement, only one party is required to appear in court. The judge signs the decree of divorce and you are free.

Keeping Your Spouse as a Friend

How important is it for you to remain on speaking terms with your soon-to-be ex spouse? Does your idea of The Successful Divorce include maintaining that relationship? In consultation with an attorney, you may want to decide just how much that friendship is worth. How much are you willing to concede to keep the other side happy?

At a time like this, when you are your most vulnerable, the steady hand of an emotionally disinterested party who is experienced at handling divorce matters may keep you from making the mistake of a lifetime.

If your goal is to keep the divorce uncontested, do yourself a favor. Have someone simply assess your situation, inform you of your rights and advise you about various scenarios that might save you trouble in the long run.

Here's an example that I deal with everyday: If your spouse wants to keep the family business, and that business comprises 90%

of your combined net worth, turning the business over to your spouse and getting nothing in return would not be smart. It is essential to have your attorney structure an agreement that allows your spouse to keep the business and give you money for your share. When the money is paid out over time, you must secure the arrangement with something of value.

When Your Spouse Suddenly Is the Enemy

There comes a time in many divorces, an unfortunate place in the road, when communication breaks down and progress comes to a halt. This is when a divorce becomes contested and difficult. If this happens to you, contact an experienced attorney who will help you work toward The Successful Divorce. Often this point comes when you least suspect it, in the midst of negotiations that are meant to end the struggle.

To ready yourself for a contested divorce, remember that your spouse, regrettably, is now the enemy, if just for the duration of the divorce. After all, this person is trying either to take away your children or keep assets from you that you need to pay your bills, or both. You can afford to be accommodating only when you leave the courthouse with most of what you wanted in the first place.

Planning Your Divorce Strategy

"Peace through strength" was a maxim of our national policy during the Cold War. The same goes for the way you should approach divorce strategy. All contested divorces should be handled as though they were going to trial. Then if you can settle things, you are ahead of the game. If settlement efforts fail, you are prepared for the battle. Sometimes a little "saber rattling" must be done so that the other side knows you are serious. I like to say that divorces must be fought with an olive branch in one hand and a board with a rusty nail in the other hand behind your back.

Sometimes you have to let your weapons show before people will sit down and be reasonable.

CHAPTER FIVE

Mediation

Let the litigation battle commence! That should have been the battle cry when Bob and Irene Vargas decided to divorce. No two people had ever disagreed as much, even over the most trivial details. Although Bob was in the printing business, they couldn't even agree that he had purchased some antique books and magazines that rightfully belonged to him.

The Vargases' attorneys had seen their ability to battle firsthand. During their one and only settlement conference, the two of them stood across the table like rhinos about to charge, bellowing at each other. Since that meeting, their attorneys had engaged in telephone tag, with Bob calling his attorney, who called Irene's attorney, who called Irene, but she was out, so she had to call back. Then Irene's attorney called Bob's attorney, who called Bob. Then Bob realized that he was "it." He had another question, and the whole process started all over again.

With the meter running on both sides, the attorneys' bills were nearing six figures, and still they hadn't gone to trial. Soon neither side would have any money left and the animosity would be so great between the parties that joint parenting of their two children would be impossible.

It's the Latest Thing

Mediation was conceived for such people as Bob and Irene. Also known as "alternative dispute resolution" or "assisted negotiation," mediation involves communication and compromise triumphing over conflict. And that's crucial for people who will have to continue a relationship, such as being parents or the owners of a family business.

The mediation process has become more popular over the past decade. In most cases, it's less expensive to mediate than litigate. If you must have a relationship with the other side after the divorce, usually a mediated settlement beats the adversarial nature of court hands down.

Explaining the Process

Just moving the process away from the courthouse and into the mediator's office often reduces the adversarial tension inherent in a divorce. The job of a divorce lawyer in court is to win for the client. The job of a divorce lawyer in mediation is to negotiate the best deal for the client within the context of an agreement that will hold up over time.

In most cases, the actual mediation process begins with the parties and their representatives — attorneys, accountants, financial planners or brokers — meeting in the same room. Here the mediator lays out the ground rules in 15 to 30 minutes of explanation. Then the parties are separated and the mediator begins a day of shuttle diplomacy, moving from room to room highlighting points of agreement, attempting to smooth over any disagreements and helping the parties come up with creative ways to resolve the case.

The best mediators are very effective at getting people to look toward common goals over the long term. Once an agreement is reached, a document called a Rule 11 Stipulation or mediated settlement agreement is prepared and signed by the parties and their attorneys. From this document, the attorneys draft a decree of divorce which is signed by the judge and the divorce is complete.

For Most Texans, It's Mandatory

Mediation is the single most significant change in family law in the past 25 years. Of about 2,240 family courts in this country, perhaps 200 offer (or require) mediation in child custody disputes. [5] This change from litigation to mediation has been prompted by the overcrowding of court dockets and a rising concern that making divorce an adversarial process is not in the best interest of children.

One mediation practice on the West Coast reports that for divorces mediated over an 11-year period, 92 percent were settled and didn't go to court. Of those mediated settlements, 89 percent still remain in force. [6]

Texas has the most progressive and intense use of mediation in the country. In 1987, four of the seven family district court judges in Dallas County began to order mandatory mediation in all divorce cases. Since then, most Texas courts have begun to require mediation before a family law case can be scheduled for trial.

Beware of Mediation Abusers

Critics of the mediation process often ask how you mediate with a spouse who is sexually abusing your kids? How do you reach a fair settlement when one side is hiding assets? How do you trust a spouse who has been carrying on an extramarital affair for 10 years?

Mediation under these circumstances can be very difficult. The truth is that mediation can be abused by a party who is not negotiating in good faith. That's why you need an attorney as your representative and adviser. But I've seen clients go into mediation skeptical of the other side's motives and still come out with a worthwhile settlement. Remember that in mediation, as in all aspects of divorce work, you lead with the olive branch and keep the rusty nail ready. You truly want to extend the olive branch, and have it accepted. But you keep the board with the rusty nail handy, just in case.

Remember the Children

In her book THE ARGUMENT CULTURE, linguist Deborah Tannen suggests there should be an alternative to the supposition that a winner and a loser must always emerge in every case that goes before the court. [7]

> "The American legal system is a prime example of trying to solve problems by pitting two sides against each other and letting them slug it out in public. It reflects and reinforces our assumption that truth emerges when two polarized, warring extremes are set against each other."

Truth and justice, as it applies to divorce, may be a matter of degrees, rather than a black and white certainty. In other types of civil litigation, the adversarial system may work perfectly. But in those instances, the warring parties haven't had children together.

Mediation allows you and your spouse to reach an acceptable compromise between differing views of truth and justice. This benefits your children and lets both sides win. And it may be the most effective pathway to The Successful Divorce.

What You Gonna Believe:
Me or Your Lyin' Ears?

"Sometimes in the courtroom, people get a perception of things that flies in the face of reality. In a child custody trial where I represented the father, things were pretty even until the other side introduced tape recordings, made by the wife, of conversations between herself and my client. She felt they showed just what a sorry guy my client was. Only these recordings didn't convey the message the wife thought they would.

"In reality, these recordings confirmed to the jury what a difficult person *she* was. After it was all over and we had won, I polled the jury and they confirmed that these tape recordings — which the other side considered their smoking guns — were the most compelling evidence in favor of my client."

Kevin Fuller
Dallas

Part Two

Pretrial: Sharpening Your Instruments

CHAPTER SIX

Winning at Trial Begins Early

Patience is a virtue that's usually not in great supply during divorce. That's why John was such an unusual client. For almost a year, unknown to his wife, the Austin stockbroker planned the breakup very carefully. It was not money that he was after with all of his scheming, but rather custody of his young son. John was convinced his wife was an unfit mother, due to mental instability. For a full year, John chronicled his wife's eccentricities, her lack of involvement in their son's life, her inattention to the needs of their family.

John decided that she could have most of their money. It was his son that concerned him. All of his planning paid off when he was awarded sole custody of the boy.

Assert Your Rights

How aggressively you pursue your divorce and how long you actually plan your escape is always subject to debate. Few divorces require a year of planning. If you are too obsessed with your mission, you can possibly alienate someone you've lived with and loved as well as those around you. But if you move into divorce with little forethought, you may be setting yourself up for a lifelong disaster.

Given the two choices and the dire consequences of inaction, assertive action will help you achieve The Successful Divorce.

Talk to your attorney about the things you have that you value most. If a certain piece of personal property is yours, get it out of the house. If your spouse is abusing you or your children, and you have proof, let your attorney advise you on how to protect your family. Your attorney needs to know where you are having problems. That's the only way the divorce can be handled to your satisfaction.

Prenuptial Agreements

For those who think about the possibility of disaster far ahead, premarital agreements or "prenups" are a perfectly reasonable response. Prenups are most popular with people who enter a marriage with large assets. Some of these assets are not easily divisible, such as an interest in a family owned business or a large tract of real estate. The original investment, under most conditions, would be separate property and not subject to division.

Any appreciation on that investment during the marriage also is generally separate property. The party who had the prenuptial agreement drawn up will want to have an original of the document in his or her possession for safekeeping. For the other party to the marriage, reversing the terms or "breaking" the prenup is very difficult.

Prenuptial agreements have gotten so much press lately that even people with modest holdings sometimes draw up papers so that a split would be made less messy. Your attorney can advise you on the use and validity of prenuptial agreements.

Sock Away Information

Most married couples include what I call a "documented" spouse and an "undocumented" one. The documented spouse usually makes most of the money, pays the bills and keeps the records. The undocumented spouse has little to do with family records, and that spouse is at a distinct disadvantage at the beginning of a divorce case.

Think of yourself as an information magnet in the early days of your divorce. Information that can make or break your case at trial is kept at the marital residence. You have to secure that information, so your spouse won't spring it on you at trial or make it hard to get.

The most relevant items include three to five years of the following:

- Personal or corporate tax returns
- Checking, savings and money market account statements
- Paid bills
- Investment account statements
- Stock or bond certificates
- Mortgage information
- Credit card information
- Information on debts and other liabilities
- Long-distance telephone bills
- Cellular telephone bills
- Medical records
- Health insurance policies

- Life insurance policies
- Family photos
- Photo evidence of extramarital affairs
- "Love" letters or other communication between your spouse and a third party
- Evidence of any other "secrets" of yours or your spouse

The idea isn't to destroy this documentation, but merely to put it away for safekeeping. It might be pertinent if used at trial, and it might not. But you want the opportunity to make that decision.

Obtaining this information does not assure you of winning most of the marital assets or gaining custody of your children. The facts of your case will dictate whether this information can be used by or against you at trial. But if you hold most of your family's information in your possession prior to trial, you control the situation.

Obtain Financial Records

Bank account records normally show a wealth of information, and often they contain facts and figures that only one of the marriage partners knows. For example, most people get paid twice a month, so there would be deposits to a checking account, customarily, on the first and 15th of each month. What if your spouse claims a monthly income of $10,000 but deposits of $25,000 are made into the checking account each month? This may indicate large commissions or bonuses received on a regular basis. You need to know about that additional income. How is the money being used? Could this indicate the existence of another relationship or perhaps a gambling problem?

In one case, we suspected the husband was hiding money but we couldn't prove it. Everything looked clean, maybe too clean. After much searching, we were looking at canceled checks and happened to notice where they were deposited. An account number on the back of one check didn't ring any bells. When we checked our list of accounts, the account wasn't on hubby's list. A trickle of money turned into a torrent when we issued a subpoena for the records of that account. In this way, we discovered a separate set of books and a lot of hidden money.

Spying, Sneaking and Snooping

Information obtained through investigation can become devastatingly effective pieces of evidence. Long-distance and cellular telephone records are great examples. Just after your spouse has told the judge that he or she is practically broke, you bring forth an enlarged phone statement with page after page of cellular calls to the same mystery number. Is this how your spouse's income gets spent each month?

Were these calls to a person of the opposite sex? A bookie? A drug connection? The best divorce lawyers will request both personal and business cellular phone and long-distance records for the past three to five years. If a spouse has been hiding these calls behind business accounts, the information will prove valuable and the guilty spouse may want to settle the case to keep an employer from finding out about those extracurricular activities.

Getting your spouse "dead to rights" is the effective part. But too often, people operate on a hunch, suspecting something but not being able to prove it. That proof is the divider between whether your information is effective or not. If you can't prove it, your information doesn't really exist and shouldn't be used in court.

Presenting potentially damaging information without solid proof just makes you look vindictive and deceitful. The decision whether to present certain evidence is not an easy one to make. This decision has to be made in the context of the overall strategy of your case.

Tell Your Attorney Everything

The combination of an experienced attorney and a helpful client is the most powerful weapon you can have in a divorce case. If you suspect something about your spouse, tell your attorney. He or she should know how to prove it, and whether the information is useful if proven. This is the value of an experienced family law specialist.

I've been in and out of courtrooms so much over the past two decades that usually I can anticipate how a certain judge or jury will view a piece of evidence, what constitutes proof for them and how much information is too much.

The only way for an attorney and his client to work together is to be totally honest with each other. From the client's perspective, you don't want to have an attorney you are afraid to tell certain things. You have every right, as a client, to expect that your attorney is able to edit the things he says and does, so that you don't have to be careful about what you tell him.

From the attorney's perspective, you want a client who is completely truthful, and whose suspicions about the other side are grounded in fact and are not simply flights of fancy.

I Know, You're Perfect

The most difficult, but essential, information to convey to your attorney are the secrets of *your* life. No one is perfect, and there's nothing you could say that most family law specialists haven't heard in the past. But still, admitting fault can be painful.

Most of this evidence is already known to your spouse, such as health or financial problems or your attitudes about sex or religion. Some of the most innocuous information can become evidence, especially if the custody of children is concerned.

There may be deep dark secrets, in your heart of darkness, that make you uncomfortable. They are secrets your spouse doesn't know about now, but can easily discover if given a chance.

This may involve an arrest for some youthful indiscretion or sexual peccadillo, a brief fling with drug abuse or some other walk on the wild side. The most common of these secrets is adultery.

Plenty of people engage in affairs and swear there is no way anyone can discover their secrets. Then they get all moon-eyed like lovestruck teenagers and do the dumbest things. They show up at the same restaurants they take their families to, but this time in the company of others. They write love letters or take photographs and leave them in a briefcase or purse. Sometimes they buy lingerie or sexual devices using a credit card.

One client was foolish enough to write checks for his girlfriend's bills from the account he and his wife used. He even wrote the other woman's name and the use of the check on the memo line. When he denied an adulterous relationship and said he didn't know anyone with the other person's name, those checks told a different story.

If you are in the midst of a divorce and you are having an affair, the best advice I can give you is to stop it at once. Let's face it, you are going to get caught, either by your spouse or a private investigator. An amazing number of people continue seeing a paramour even when they realize their spouse is watching like a hawk. Sometimes you would think the person is trying to get caught, because he or she is so blatantly foolish. Very few extramarital relationships are worth the check you will have to write to settle the divorce when your secret becomes known.

You also have to understand the strain you put everyone under by continuing this other relationship, as if the tension relating to divorce wasn't enough. And if your marriage includes children, you are in danger of affecting their psychological well-being with such reckless actions.

The law gives parents the benefit of the doubt, asserting that, even in divorce, no one ceases to be a parent. The best thing for you to do is remember that you are a parent first. Your sex life should come second to these duties. You will remain a parent after the divorce. What you want your kids to remember is how you were forthright and available to them in this time of crisis.

Hiring a Private Investigator

Any client who impulsively hires a private investigator without consulting an attorney may be wasting time and money. The attorney usually has an investigator he trusts and recommends for your case. In certain cases, an investigator's work may be the most important evidence at hand. You can imagine the reaction of a judge or jury when you produce videotape of your spouse kissing someone he or she testifies to have never met.

Another divorce lawyer told me his investigator caught a mother, on tape, having sex in a car with someone who was not her husband. The clincher was that her baby son was sitting beside them in his car seat. Not all investigators' evidence is so compelling. The report may be repetitive and simply back up evidence you already have.

Most investigators charge by the hour, and that money is payable when the work is done. Whatever the results, you will pay handsomely for these services, and there is no guarantee that the dirt dug up on your spouse will bury him or her. A skilled family law specialist can discredit many investigators' reports, especially if there are flaws in the actions taken or a lack of experience by the investigator. As in most aspects of life as well as divorce, you get what you pay for. Hiring a competent investigator is essential.

Using Tape Recorders

You may feel that if you capture an indiscretion on tape, you have the other party dead to rights. But before you purchase a recording hookup from Radio Shack and join the CIA, be mindful that you could wind up in deep trouble. In Texas, at least one party to a conversation must know he or she is being taped. In other words, you can tape yourself talking to another person who is unaware of the intrusion. But it is a criminal offense to wiretap or tape a conversation between two or more people who don't know you are taping them.

Even discounting the legal problems inherent in the taping of conversations, getting your spouse on tape may not be as helpful as you think. Many judges look at taping as a devious form of spying on the other side, and you need to have pretty damning evidence on the tape or the judge or jury might punish you for it.

However, if you have a spouse who continually denies things that you know he or she has done, a tape recording may be the only way to establish the truth. The decision whether to use a tape recording should be made by you and your attorney after careful consideration.

CHAPTER SEVEN

Building a Winning Case

A noted jurist once said there are three sides to every divorce case — his side, her side and the truth.

For Laura, getting at the truth was difficult in her divorce. Her husband ran his own business and it was nearly impossible to determine just how much money he made. Hoping to handle this part of the divorce in a civilized manner, Laura repeatedly asked him for financial information. They discussed his financial situation at great length, and he provided her with income estimates that she considered suspiciously low. He was always civil, saying he would get her backup for his claims, but somehow it was never provided.

Soon the time came to enter substantive settlement negotiations, but still she had no documents from him. A decision had to be made in order to get this man off dead center. Laura and her attorney decided to ask for every check and bill as well as a list of his business customers and vendors for a period of five years. They asked him to bring all of that information to a deposition that they estimated would take at least one full day.

Within four hours, Laura received the information she originally requested and her attorney rescinded his request for the extraordinary list of documents.

This story emphasizes the he-said, she-said nature of divorce litigation and the importance of the discovery process. Discovery gives both parties the ability to obtain information from the other side concerning the relevant issues in a case. This portion of the divorce process involves either formal or informal requests for information from the opposing party. The objective is to level the playing field so both sides have access to all the information and documentation necessary to resolve a case.

Formal discovery procedures may include written interrogatories, requests for production of documents, requests for admissions, oral depositions and the exchange of inventories.

A friendly exchange of information between two people who were close at one time may seem natural. But often these procedures become intense and highly charged debates over access to information. In the most rancorous divorces, one side may have to force the other side to provide even the most basic information such as checking account statements and tax returns. It is the responsibility of your attorney to decide how important a piece of information is to your case, and to what lengths you will go to obtain it.

Only after you are fairly confident that you know the assets and liabilities involved in the divorce would you want to talk about settlement.

Interrogatories

One of the first discovery tools used in a divorce is interrogatories — written questions designed to discover certain facts. The answers to these questions are given under oath, and they must be prepared and filed within a prescribed period of time.

Since interrogatories are issued early in the process, sometimes you can catch the other side unaware of the consequences of an answer. Sometimes you can unearth an outright lie, something the judge or a jury frowns on. Those lies can have an impact on your case.

Interrogatories may include questions relating to a party's employment and salary information, bank accounts, charge accounts, assets and debts. You may be asked what persons have knowledge of the facts relating to your case. And there may be fault questions pertaining to such activities as drug abuse, spousal abuse or adultery.

Of course, you may also have to answer interrogatories. If questions are directed at you, you will need to discuss the inquiries with your attorney to determine the best way to respond.

All answers to interrogatories need to be supplemented before a trial so that the information is up to date.

Requests for Documents

A request for production of documents contains specific demands for certain documents needed for the preparation of a case. The requesting party usually wants three to five years of bank statements, tax returns, charge statements, business records, insurance information, financial data and numerous other kinds of information, including any evidence that the responding party plans to use at trial.

Documents you plan to submit at trial must be made available to the other side, if they ask for them. In most cases, if you fail to produce a document when requested, you will be prevented from using it in court. At trial, a responsible attorney will object to the admission of documents he or she has been unable to examine because the other side didn't produce them.

Requests for Admissions

In a request for admissions, a party is asked to admit or deny facts or propositions in the case. This method of discovery is used as a shortcut to determining facts in a case.

For instance, your attorney may ask the opposing party to stipulate that a piece of property is actually separate property and not part of the marital estate. Or you may be asked to admit or deny an extramarital affair during the marriage.

A guilty party is put in a delicate position when asked this question. Admitting adultery, for instance, may concede a fact the other side could have trouble proving in court. But if you deny the relationship and the other side can prove it at trial, you are not only an adulterer, but you are dishonest and potentially guilty of perjury.

Failure to answer a request for admissions in a timely manner may cause the request to be considered automatically admitted by the court. So you cannot simply avoid answering questions without additional negative consequences.

Depositions

The deposition is the most confrontational, and often most

important, part of the discovery process, since it is taken in person, under oath, often with the opposing party present. In most divorce cases, a deposition is necessary to discover the basis of the opposing party's case or the substance of the testimony of a witness in the case.

Usually your deposition will be taken in the office of one of the attorneys in the case and in the presence of a court reporter who is taking down everything you say.

Your lawyer should be present to protect your rights, but really your deposition is run by the opposing attorney, who will ask questions about the facts of the case and the history of the marriage. Your deposition may or may not break your case at trial, depending on how you testify and the particular facts of your case.

You must be prepared to name each and every reason you want the divorce, if you plan to utilize these reasons at trial. And as with the interrogatories, you are asked to name every person who has knowledge of your case. Working with your attorney, you should prepare for your deposition so you do not forget critical parts of the case under the pressure and intensity of the moment.

While you always should tell the truth, there are numerous strategies for handling a deposition, and your attorney should advise you about the impact of a particular deposition and the questions asked.

Sometimes a deposition can be a shortcut to discovering the entire case of your opposition. In a large property case several years ago, the wife of my client filed a vicious and accusatory pleading alleging much wrongdoing on the part of my client. We knew there was no evidence to back up the claims of the wife, so we insisted on taking her deposition at the very start of the case rather than waiting until after we had done other discovery. What we learned in the deposition was that the wife had no facts to support her claims against my client. Her attorneys simply filed the pleading as a tactic, hoping to put the husband on the defensive. Instead, the exact opposite occurred. The wife and her attorneys were put on the defensive and stayed there throughout the case because of a tactic gone bad.

A deposition can be used to discredit a witness who changes his or her testimony at trial. Good lawyers use the deposition process to "size up" the opposing party and their case to determine how they will appear on the witness stand. It is important to prepare for the deposition and then make notes of what was said in it for use in trial.

Often, lawyers try to trick the other side at trial by saying, "That's not what you said at your deposition." Sometimes the lawyer himself doesn't remember what the opposing party said in the deposition, but simply wants to test the witness' memory. If the lawyer believes the witness is lying, he may attempt to confuse the witness in hopes that he or she could not remember the story told in the deposition.

Often a party will use the deposition to scare the opposition, giving a taste of the confrontational atmosphere you can expect in an actual trial. This lesson can be an expensive but effective one for the person scheduling the deposition. Depositions usually require the services of a court reporter, who makes a transcript of the testimony, and a lawyer, who must spend time preparing for it. Before you decide to take the deposition of your estranged spouse or other witnesses in the case, make certain a settlement can't be reached beforehand and that the information you might get is worthwhile. Depositions can cost you from about $500 to several thousand dollars to complete.

If you want to find out about a bank account with a few hundred dollars in it, perhaps there are other ways to get the information. If you suspect the existence of an account with many thousands of dollars hidden away in it, or if custody of your children is at issue, a deposition can be a worthwhile investment.

CHAPTER EIGHT

The Tiebreaker: Who's at Fault?

Lewis was on his second divorce. The first time he went before the judge, in the early 1960s, one party to a divorce had to accuse the other party of awful conduct just to have the divorce granted. The atmosphere in the courtroom was different then. Lewis thought the whole process was cruel, having to explain and embellish all the things his wife had done, just to dissolve the marriage. Since that day, he and his first wife had not spoken. She considered him her sworn enemy, and he believed the system forced him into this terrible position.

He was certain that would not happen with this divorce. Under Texas' no-fault statute, there was no reason for people to walk away from the courthouse angry at each other.

Since 1969, when the Legislature adopted Title 1 of the Texas Family Code, this state has sanctioned no-fault divorce. Parties seeking divorce no longer have to prove improper conduct or other grounds for dissolution of the marriage. Still, this does not mean that in Texas, the cause of the divorce doesn't matter.

The Role of Fault
In a No-Fault World

You can imagine how tired family court judges get hearing about how someone's honey did them wrong. Judges would rather not deal with the issue of fault in a marriage. But with the responsibility for property division and the awarding of custody or substantial visitation, judges often get called upon to make a moral judgment of who did what to whom and, therefore, who deserves what. In other words, fault still matters. In fact, the issue of fault is more complicated than ever before.

If there is no fault present and the parties have merely grown apart, the court usually will attempt to divide the community assets and debts of the marriage in an equitable manner.

Texas is one of nine states that employs community property statutes. All property acquired during the marriage is presumed to be community property and is subject to division by the court. Most people assume that division will be equal, but that isn't what the Texas Family Code provides. The law in Texas calls for an equitable or "just and right" division of the property. The separate property of a spouse generally consists of gifts or inheritances, property that was owned by one party before the marriage, or the proceeds from the sale of a separate property asset. Separate property is not divisible by the court. However, a party who is alleging separate property ownership has the burden of proving it is separate by "clear and convincing" evidence.

If the parties cannot agree on the division of property, the judge will determine, based on the facts, what kind of division is fair and equitable. Those facts might include the length of the marriage, the ability of the parties to make a living after the divorce, the assets and debts in question and who gets the children. In some cases, who's at fault for the divorce — along with the type of fault — is the tie-breaker.

Types of Fault

Admonitions that "I divorced him because he wouldn't support my entire family" or allegations that a spouse snored too loudly might mean your expectations were not met, but they aren't what a trial judge would consider as fault in a divorce. These are examples of the types of fault we are talking about:

- Adultery
- Drug use
- Alcoholism
- Physical abuse of a spouse or child
- Mental abuse of a spouse or child
- Sexual abuse of a spouse or child
- Overly suspicious or obsessive behavior
- Gambling
- Excessive spending
- Mental illness or psychological problems
- Criminal convictions
- Unusual sexual practices
- Long absences from home

You'd Better Be Able to Prove It

Look at the list of faults. First ask yourself if your spouse evidences signs of one or more of these behaviors? We're not talking here about petty little annoyances, but acts that truly disrupt the marital union.

Often people come to the judge with such small upsets that *they,* and not the other party, are considered at fault for the divorce.

If you can list two or three things your spouse does on this list, you next have to ask yourself if you can prove it. You've seen how people can clean up their act for court. One of the prime examples in recent years was Michael Fortier, the Arizona man who was friends with Timothy McVeigh, the convicted Oklahoma City bomber.

Fortier, by all accounts, was a drug abuser and a man of dubious character. But by the time he made his way to court, he looked like a tenured math professor who could not tell a lie. Anyone who had seen a photo of him before his court date would swear this was a different person.

The point is that you can't expect your spouse to walk into court looking like he did the last time he beat the children. Most likely, he won't admit his failings and throw himself on the mercy of the court.

You must be able to prove in court whatever you allege. That proof can be witnesses — yourself and others. It can be a paper trail of receipts, bank withdrawals and the like. It can even be photographs, video and audio recordings. But there must be proof, or you can come out looking like one vindictive spouse.

The courts often utilize what is called a "reasonable person's standard," based on all of the evidence. The judge often considers whether the evidence indicates the behavior of a married person properly executing familial duties. Most people in successful marriages are not seen in bars late at night with another person of the opposite sex. They are not at that person's apartment several times each week. And they don't make hundreds of cellular phone calls to the person late at night. In this type of situation, most divorce lawyers put the burden on the accused party to explain all of these circumstances. Remember, your judge probably will be married and have a keen sense of what actions are reasonable in a marriage.

If you are guilty of marital misconduct, you need to consider how your actions will look. You and your lawyer can decide how to handle these issues. If you are not guilty, you and your lawyer must decide how to combat the misconceptions.

Again, if you think your spouse is guilty of an indiscretion, you need to develop concrete proof to establish guilt and not just rely on speculation and rumor, which are not admissible as evidence in court.

CHAPTER NINE

Coping with Domestic Violence

If you look at the situation statistically, domestic violence is epidemic in this country. According to the National Coalition Against Domestic Violence, 20,000 deaths resulting from domestic violence occur each year. [8]

Shockingly, domestic violence is the number one cause of injury to women in this country — more than automobile accidents, rapes and muggings combined. In these cases, divorce may be the only avenue of escape. For many people, the first step is to admit that you are in an abusive relationship. The second and most important step is to prove to the divorce court judge that abuse is happening.

Child Abuse: Divorce Complaint of the 1980s

In the late 1980s, the old bias in favor of women in child custody cases began to fade. So inventive attorneys concocted a new strategy to combat the growing number of fathers who were gaining custody of their children. They cried child abuse by the fathers. At once, the system recoiled like a snake. The mere allegation of abuse was enough to cut daddy off from his kids and endanger his very freedom. Certainly, in some cases, the abuse was real. But in others, it was a clear example of certain parties using a hot button issue to extract settlements they otherwise would not get.

By now, judges and juries have heard child abuse claims in conjunction with divorce so many times that this is a highly suspect strategy. Finders of fact look suspiciously at parents who make their first allegation of physical or sexual abuse immediately after a divorce complaint has been filed. So why had that parent never taken any action about those concerns until a divorce was in the works? So many parents have lied about abuse that legitimate cases must meet a standard of proof that's often impossible to attain. Judges are adamant that you prove abuse beyond a doubt.

Signs of Physical Abuse

The most common signs of physical abuse are:

- Does your spouse hit or kick you?
- Do you get threatened with guns or other weapons?
- Do you endure screaming or threats?
- Does your spouse break items in your house?
- Do you have to submit to forced sex?
- Does your spouse threaten to harm you if you leave?

If any of the above happen to you, take action immediately to protect yourself and your children. If you feel threatened, leave the situation. Stay with family members, friends or in a shelter until you can obtain relief in court. And if you have to leave, do everything possible to take your children with you. When the dust settles, get professional help to explain your options.

Documenting Abuse

For both you and your children, documenting abuse is essential. This can be done with sound medical evidence, including doctors' reports and photographs. A photograph of a bruised face is the most powerful evidence you can present at trial.

Evidence like this should be backed up by the testimony of your doctor or the child's pediatrician. He or she can be a great source of immediate assistance and can direct you to other professional help. If your doctor believes that child abuse is indicated, state law requires that this abuse be reported to Child Protective Services, a branch of the Texas Department of Protective and Regulatory Services.

That agency will act according to certain laws, and may require that the child be taken away from the source of the endangerment. Your actions may start a chain reaction that you cannot stop once you seek professional help. You need to have made all the necessary preparations to deal with what will follow, including seeking sound legal advice concerning a divorce.

Involving the Authorities

When you feel threatened, by all means call the police. They can immediately intervene to help you. If you are facing a choice of calling the police or leaving, leave and then call them from a safe location. If the police believe they have enough evidence, they can arrest your spouse on the scene. The police may, however, ask you to press charges against your spouse. This process usually involves you swearing to the offense before a magistrate in the jurisdiction where the abuse occurred. Once the warrant has been issued, the police will arrest your spouse and the case will be set for trial.

Please be aware, however, that this is a very lengthy and involved process. If it is a first offense, the court may recommend counseling rather than jail time. The sooner you start to establish a history of this type of behavior, the more likely the court will put that spouse in jail for repeated incidents.

Statistics show that a woman is abused in the United States every 15 seconds. If you are in this type of situation, you need to seek help immediately, before the situation escalates to a potentially fatal situation. The great lesson learned by the O.J. Simpson case is that domestic violence is real, and it can happen in every kind of family situation.

The most traumatic type of case we deal with involves sexual abuse of a young child by a parent, a close family member or a friend. Cases like this can happen to your child and require immediate action. Remember that child abuse can occur in any type of racial, ethnic, religious or economic group, even in the wealthiest of families.

Divorce Recovery Classes

Over the years, our perception of child abuse has changed dramatically. What was once corporal punishment is now considered child abuse by many in the social science community.

Actions that take place between parents and in the family during divorce are increasingly thought to be a form of child abuse. For that reason, there is a nationwide trend toward instruction for parents and children that lessens the rigors of divorce.

Churches, nonprofit social service agencies and private therapeutic practices all over the country have designed programs to address that need. Customarily, clients attend weekly classes and support groups during the most difficult period of a divorce. Usually, children meet with other children under the guidance of a trained professional counselor to discuss their feelings and the problems they face with divorce. At the same time, parents meet with other parents and get information about how the situations are affecting the kids.

In Dallas, several programs are in operation, including those sponsored by the Dallas Child Guidance Clinic and by EXCAP, the Exchange Club Center for the Prevention of Child Abuse. Family district court judges in Dallas County refer families to these programs and have made attendance in such programs mandatory for anyone with children who is seeking a divorce in their courts. These programs don't discourage divorce, although most of the people associated with divorce recovery applaud the recent trend toward a lower divorce rate.

Every major city in Texas has some type of divorce recovery program. If you live in a rural area, you might have trouble finding a program. But most judges and court-appointed social workers can guide you toward one.

Bev Bradburn-Stern, who developed the nationwide Children Cope With Divorce program used by EXCAP, wrote in the CCWD newsletter that what hurts children is not the existence of conflict between parents, but the ways conflict is expressed. "Parents, preoccupied by constant interpersonal hostility, simply cannot put sufficient energy into their parenting roles. It is the resulting disruption of parenting that most harms children, whether or not a divorce occurs. This differs significantly from the impact of periodic episodes of mild conflict." [9]

In a Market of Bulls and Bears, This Is Some Dog

"In a case I mediated, the husband and wife were both employed and had a fairly substantial community estate. However, they seemed far more interested in ownership of their mutt, Diablo. Each party told me early in the mediation that they would not settle unless they got the dog. I told them that we would first divide the property and then we would conduct an auction for the dog.

"Part of the property settlement provided for splitting an $11,000 tax refund. When the bidding began, the wife offered to give her share of the tax refund ($5,500) for the dog. The husband rejected the bid and offered his share of the tax refund and upped the bid by $5,000, a total of $10,500. The wife rejected the bid and offered the tax refund and upped the bid by $10,000. At that juncture, the husband blinked, took the $15,500, fell out of love with the dog, and the wife waltzed away with her valuable pooch. Both parties were very, very happy."

Harry Tindall
Houston

Part Three
Who Gets What?

CHAPTER TEN

In the Best Interest of the Children

The last thing Don wanted from the divorce was his children. At least that's what he thought when it all started. During the marriage, his wife had been a stay-at-home mom. She took the kids to the doctor and was present at school parties and church activities. Don thought of himself only as the provider for his family, although he coached his son's baseball team. And increasingly, it seemed that he served as a referee in spats between his wife and their daughter.

It was only after the tension between himself and his wife reached epic proportions — when he moved out of their Amarillo home — that he decided he couldn't just give up his children.

He began to reevaluate his relationship with his children. Since his wife was so high-strung, they came to him when they really needed to talk. And as time went along, friends told him how distant his wife had been with the kids.

So he became determined that he wouldn't just walk away. Gaining custody of his children might be out of the question, but at least when they were older he could say he tried. He could start by trying to get his wife to agree to joint custody. If that couldn't be accomplished by agreement, perhaps a judge or jury would agree that joint custody was the proper situation for this family.

Then it would just be a waiting game, to see if his wife was up to the task of taking care of their children. And if she wasn't, going for custody might not be such an impossibility.

Custody: The Fight of Your Life

There are many reasons why divorcing parents fight each other for custody of their children. Pride often enters into it. Revenge is a motive in some cases. I've seen parents file for custody simply to gain a bargaining chip in the fight for the marital assets. But most of the time, people contest custody because they sincerely believe that the children are better off with them than with the other parent.

The history of child custody has been an interesting one, with the pendulum swinging radically one way then the other. Back when divorce first became legal in Texas, children were considered the property of the man, just like almost everything else. Since the man had all the assets, how could the woman possibly take care of the children? So they were, most often, left with their father.

In the early 20th century, women won the right to vote along with a steady increase in the overall level of their rights. No longer were they the property of their husbands. With increases in the number of divorces, women gained a special status in relation to their children. When custody was an issue, women automatically kept the children unless the father could prove something awful about the mother that made her unfit to care for her children in the eyes of the community.

This standard continued until the late 1970s, especially with the custody of young children. Today, men are gaining custody of the kids with increasing frequency. Changing social mores have a lot to do with that. More households have two wage earners, and so the care of children is increasingly shared between the parents. Judges are more amenable to men as primary caregivers. And since Texas is the only state where you can have a jury in a custody trial, many men here feel they can roll the dice and possibly win in court.

Each child custody case is unique due to the facts, circumstances and fault surrounding the breakup of the marriage, as well as each parent's individual relationship with the children during and after the marriage.

In most cases, the parent's role with the children after the divorce mirrors their relationship before the divorce. If the marriage was a traditional one, where the father spent less time with the children than his wife did prior to the divorce, it is doubtful that he would instantly become heavily involved in the children's lives. If this was a two-wage-earner family, both mother and father probably had their absentee periods. During and after the divorce, it is likely that this relationship would continue. Sometimes, there is a period of intense activity by the father during the divorce, giving rise to the term "Disneyland dad." Then the lives of parents and children settle into what they will be over the long haul.

Despite what caused the divorce, the children are not at fault for the breakup and deserve to have the best relationship possible with both parents after the divorce. In addition, statistics clearly indicate that the parent without primary custody is more likely to pay child support and help with other expenses related to the child if he or she sees the children regularly.

Types of Custody

Whether custody is agreed upon or awarded by the court, there are two types of custody in Texas: sole custody and joint custody. Your rights under the different custody arrangements can vary greatly. Under a sole custody arrangement, one parent has the legal right to the care, custody and control of the minor children. The other parent is awarded specific visitation rights with the children. This means the children will live with the parent who is awarded sole custody. That parent typically has the right — and the responsibility — to make all major decisions related to the children, including establishing the children's primary residence and all medical, educational, academic and social matters.

Under a joint custody arrangement, one parent usually is designated the primary custodian, although joint custody means the sharing of certain parental rights and duties. Joint custody does not mean that each parent will have possession of the children 50% of the time. The children live with the primary custodian except for the time they are with the other parent under a specified schedule. Joint custody arrangements must specify what decisions are made by which parent.

The Law Favors Joint Custody

Joint custody has been a part of Texas family law for years, but once it was considered suitable only for divorcing parents who could settle disputes surrounding their children in a civilized manner. Consequently, it was ordered only when both parties asked for it.

In 1987, the Texas Legislature amended the family code to allow

judges and juries to consider joint custody in all cases involving children, even when there was no agreement between the parents. Now
parents who cannot stand the sight of each other can be forced to
work out differences for the sake of their children. This provision
allows both parents to retain some control over their children's lives
and it alleviates the stigma many parents feel when they give up custody of their children or have it taken away by the courts.

Over the last several years, the Texas Legislature has modified
the Family Code so that many features of joint custody are similar to
sole custody. For instance, when parents with joint custody cannot
agree on the major issues in a child's life — academics, medical treatment and others — one party may have veto power over the other to
resolve disputes. The parent with the final authority on a particular
issue may override the other parent's request every time and this veto
power can create tremendous conflict between the parents. For example, the primary custodial parent may retain final authority over
academic decisions, while the other parent may only voice an opinion about academic decisions. If a dispute arises concerning whether
the children attend public or private school, the parent with the authority over such decisions has the right to make the final decision.

Joint custody tends to push parents together in a sense of cooperation. I've seen parents who were fighting like Bengal tigers wise
up and begin to cooperate for their children's sake under the terms
of a joint custody arrangement.

I've also seen the label of joint custody foster a misunderstand-
ing between parents because they don't understand their legal rights.
It is important for people to know that simply because it is joint
custody, both parents do not retain a 50/50 vote in the decisions concerning the children.

The access arrangement is agreed upon by the parties or set by the judge.

Whether joint custody is agreed upon or ordered by the judge or jury, the court must either restrict the domicile of the child to a particular county or designate which parent has the right to determine the child's legal residence. Domicile restrictions are becoming more common. The courts recognize that if the primary parent moves the child to another state, there goes the close relationship between the other parent and the kids. Only if the primary parent provides a compelling reason for needing to move the child away from the other parent will the court allow the move.

Joint custody also does not mean you can forego payment of child support. Support is based on the needs of the children and the income of the parents.

Joint custody is generally a good thing that does not fit every situation. It can be a great thing for children if it means keeping contact with two good parents.

Sample Joint Custody Language

The following language contains the typical terms contained in a joint custody agreement, written just as it might be in your decree of divorce. Pay particular attention to this language and how it might apply to everyday life:

The Court, having considered the circumstances of the parents and of the children, finds that the following orders are in the best interest of the children.

It is ordered that John Doe and Mary Doe are appointed Managing Conservators of the following children: Sarah Doe and Thomas Doe.

It is ordered that, at all times, John Doe and Mary Doe, as Joint Managing Conservators, shall each have the following rights and duty:

1. the right to receive information from the other parent concerning the health, education and welfare of the children;

2. the duty to inform the other parent in a timely manner of significant information concerning the health, education and welfare of the children;

3. the right to confer with the other parent to the extent possible before making a decision concerning the health, education and welfare of the children;

4. the right of access to medical, dental, psychological and educational records of the children;

5. the right to consult with a physician, dentist or psychologist of the children;

6. the right to consult with school officials concerning the children's welfare and educational status, including school activities;

7. the right to attend school activities;

8. the right to be designated on the children's records as a person to be notified in case of an emergency;

9. the right to consent to medical, dental and surgical treatment during an emergency involving an immediate danger to the health and safety of the children; and

It is ordered that, during their respective periods of possession, John Doe and Mary Doe, as Joint Managing Conservators, shall each have the following rights and duties:

1. the duty of care, control, protection and reasonable discipline of the children;

2. the duty to support the children, including providing the children with clothing, food, shelter and medical and dental care not involving an invasive procedure;

3. the right to consent for the children to medical and dental care not involving an invasive procedure;

4. the right to direct the moral and religious training of the children.

It is ordered that John Doe, as a Joint Managing Conservator, shall have the following rights and duty;

1. the right to consent to medical, dental and surgical treatment involving invasive procedures and to consent to psychiatric and psychological treatment of the children;

2. the right to represent the children in legal action and to make other decisions of substantial legal significance concerning the children;

3. the right to consent to marriage and to enlistment in the armed forces of the United States;

4. the right to the services and earnings of the children;

5. except when a guardian of the children's estates or a guardian or attorney ad litem has been appointed for the children, the right to act as an agent of the children in relation to the children's estates if the children's actions are required by a state, the United States or a foreign government; and

6. the duty to manage the estates of the children to the extent created by Petitioner, John Doe, or his family; Petitioner shall continue to manage the trust containing real property at no expense to Respondent.

It is ordered that Mary Doe, as a Joint Managing Conservator, shall have the following rights and duty:

1. the right to consent to medical, dental and surgical treatment involving invasive procedures and to consent to psychiatric and psychological treatment of the children;

2. the right to receive and give receipt for periodic payments for the support of the children and to hold or disburse these funds for the benefit of the children;

3. the right to represent the children in legal action and to make other decisions of substantial legal significance concerning the children;

4. the right to consent to marriage and to enlistment in the armed forces of the United States;

5. the right to the services and earnings of the children; and

6. the duty to manage the estates of the children to the extent created by Respondent, Mary Doe, or her family; Petitioner shall continue to manage the trust containing real property at no expense to Respondent.

It is ordered that the primary residence of the children shall be in Dallas County or a county contiguous thereto ("Domicile area") and the parties shall not remove the children from the Domicile area thereto for the purpose of changing the primary residence of the children until modified by further order of the court of continuing jurisdiction or by written agreement signed by the parties and filed with the court. It is further ordered that John Doe shall have exclusive right to establish the children's primary residence within the Domicile area.

Most joint custody agreements contain language like this, with modifications as needed to fit the everyday life of the children and the parents.

When Is Sole Custody Appropriate?

Although there is a presumption in favor of joint custody in Texas courts, there are circumstances where sole custody is the only real option. This may occur under the following conditions:

- When one parent is completely absent or drops out of sight.
- When one parent is unwilling to share responsibility for the children or cooperate in the making of decisions on their behalf.
- When one parent is unable to participate in decision making due to some form of incapacity.
- When one parent is proved to have harmed the children or the other spouse either physically, mentally or sexually.
- When the enmity between two parents is considered so great that to force them to cooperate could be injurious to the children.

Who Should Be the Primary Custodian?

In a custody dispute, it is important to illustrate to the court that one parent has been the primary custodian of the child during the marriage. This parent often is the one who receives primary custody of the child after the divorce, unless there are significant conflicting circumstances or certain problems with that parent. To determine who has been the primary custodian, you need to determine who performs most of the following activities for the child:

- Who helps the child get dressed for school?

- Who fixes breakfast for the child?
- Who packs the child's lunch for school?
- Who helps the child with homework?
- Who participates in school activities with the child?
- Who takes care of the child after school?
- Who bathes the child?
- Who takes the child to the doctor?
- Who takes the child shopping?
- Who takes the child to religious activities?
- Who arranges for the child's extracurricular activities?
- Who helps the child in various stages of development?
- Who nurtures the child?

It is also important for the judge or jury to know about changes that will take place in the household after the marriage. For instance, the mother might have been a homemaker during the marriage. When the divorce is final, she may be forced to work outside the home. The relative abilities of husband and wife to parent may be significantly altered.

What a Parent Should Know About a Child Before a Custody Battle

Here's a test you can give yourself concerning the care of your child. Any parent who has participated in the majority of the activities outlined above should be able to answer most of the following questions:

- Who is the child's doctor?

- Where is the doctor's office?
- What allergies does the child have?
- Who is the child's dentist?
- Who is the child's principal?
- Who is the child's teacher?
- What is the child's favorite subject in school?
- Who is the child's day care provider?
- How often does the child go to day care?
- Name the child's three best friends.
- What is the child's favorite book?
- What is the child's favorite color?
- What special needs does the child have?
- What size shoe does the child wear?
- What clothing size does the child wear?

Sometimes a parent who means well, but hasn't taken an active role in the child care, needs time to establish a role with the child and learn these things about the child before asking for custody. One client was convinced his wife was mentally unstable and could not care for their children anymore. Although he had worked long hours and traveled for his company, he was determined to change all of that after the divorce. For months, he strengthened his position with the children and kept a journal of his wife's erratic behavior.

After a particularly disturbing weekend at home, the father alerted us to file the divorce, and he moved the children elsewhere for the child's protection. Because he had prepared so well and could show how his wife's mental state was affecting his kids, the man won sole custody of the children and the wife received a safe amount of visitation.

Custody/Visitation Problems Are Numerous

"I always tell my son the truth. I think it is important that he knows his mother is a fat alcoholic." This straight-faced declaration by the father of a 5-year-old speaks volumes about the visitation problems this divorced family will have in the future.

Children — especially young children — often become entangled in their parents' problems with each other. If young children are involved in the divorce, you can almost guarantee visitation problems in the future. No settlement agreement can address all of the potential circumstances that arise in the raising of children. Disputes may involve the simplest of issues, from a parent who cannot pick up the child at a scheduled time due to unforeseen circumstances, to a child who has an important event during a visitation period and the noncustodial parent refuses to take the child to the event.

Clients occasionally call us in a panic because an ex-spouse was 10 minutes late returning a child from visitation. One family district court judge asked the attorneys involved in this visitation dispute if their clients had lost their minds. In many instances, clients do feel they are losing their minds because of all the emotions involved. Why would anyone get the court involved over such a trivial violation of a court order? The truth is that the problems you experience during and after divorce are magnified, sometimes beyond all reason. Plenty of married couples run late. Yet, when a court order spells out a visitation schedule, parents sometimes believe there are absolutely no exceptions to the rule. Sometimes being late is a form of rebellion for a noncustodial parent who is unhappy with the arrangement. And complaining about the lateness is a way for custodial parents to criticize the actions of an ex-mate.

I've seen parents who were not allowed to take a child to sport-ing events because the games were not during a visitation period. Even worse, the mother may tell the child, "I would like to let you go to the game, but I can't trust your father to bring you home on time." The child is denied an opportunity to be with the other parent and is placed in the middle of a visitation dispute.

Standard Access

The court tries to stabilize children, sometimes at the expense of the parents' comfort, often by setting up a standard possession order (called "standard access"). Some primary custodial parents have problems allowing the other parent to have even this minimum visitation with the children. But by establishing a specific visitation schedule, the courts attempt to diffuse visitation problems and en-sure that children have plenty of access to both parents.

The court wants to foster the relationship of the children with the noncustodial parent. Unless you can prove that seeing this par-ent will harm the children, usually the judge will not limit the non-custodial parent's visitation to less than the standard access. The court generally provides different schedules when parents live less than or more than 100 miles apart, and there are provisions for alter-ations in the schedule. The standard possession order is listed in the appendix to this book. You should consult your attorney for the specific language applicable to you.

Keeping Both Parents in Their Lives

In most cases, children in a divorce deserve an equivalent amount of guidance from both parents. The children did not cause or deserve the divorce, and they are entitled to have two parents who don't use them as pawns against each other. Parents may say they are just being honest with their children when they are simply trying to turn the children against the other parent by filling the children's heads with negative images.

One of my cases involved a mother who talked so badly about the father all week long that when it came time for his weekend visitation, the children didn't want to go with their father. The mother said she could not understand why the children would not go. Eventually, it was shown that the mother said so many negative things about the father that the children truly believed he was a monster. The mother would give the children a tape recorder to record their father, since she believed he always lied to them. These children would pick up the phone when their father called and begin recording. Or they would turn the recorder on whenever he came to the door to pick them up.

The father was, in fact, a fine person and a good father. When he sued for custody, the children testified that they loved their father very much, but they did not want to hurt their mother's feelings by going with their father. So they just didn't go on the visitation. The mother was found in contempt of court for willfully violating the court's order set forth in the divorce decree and was sentenced to jail. Occasionally, mothers who act this way lose custody of their children. This mother not only taught the children to lie, but she also created a barrier that nearly destroyed the father's relationship with them. If not for the father's persistence, he likely would have had to give up on his children altogether.

This shows the horrible way children can be used as pawns during and after a divorce. There are always differences of opinion over who is the better parent, but those disputes should be between the parents. As a rule, I put a child on the witness stand only when the client and I have made a decision that, due to the overwhelming need for the testimony, we have no other choice. An example would be if the child was the only witness to a particularly abusive incident.

Lawyers who put a child on the stand merely to ask which parent he or she wants to live with are taking a huge risk with the well-being of the child and the viability of the case. It's a strategy judges and juries often won't forgive. Many times I question whether the parties and their lawyers know the destructive power they hold and the damage they can do by involving a child in this manner.

How much your children are harmed by the divorce depends largely on how you handle it. Your children will always remember this period in their lives. If you neglect them, they will never forget it. If you use them as pawns, they will realize it, today or in the future. One day they will grow up and the games their parents played with their lives will become more apparent. The only winning course for a parent is to do what is in the best interest of the children. To do otherwise would harm not only your children, but your own self-worth.

A Chronology
of Family Law in Texas

1841

The Divorce Act of 1841 establishes the first grounds for divorce in the Texas Republic.

1945

A record number of divorces takes place when millions of American men return from service in World War II to women who have tasted the independence of working in war-related industries. Many want to continue working, leading to our first crisis of family values.

1969

The Texas Legislature adopts Title 1 of the Texas Family Code, allowing no-fault divorce.

1972

Houston physician Dr. John Hill, who was acquitted of murdering his first wife, is himself murdered shortly after divorcing his second wife. These events inspire BLOOD AND MONEY, the bestselling nonfiction crime book.

1975

The Texas Board of Legal Specialization begins to certify attorneys as family law specialists.

1987

The Texas Legislature amends the Family Code to allow judges and juries to consider joint custody in all cases involving children. The same year, four family district court judges in Dallas County become the first in the state to order mandatory mediation in all divorce and child custody cases.

1988

Dallas real estate developer Robert Edelman is sentenced to federal prison for attempting to hire a hit man to kill his wife during their divorce proceedings. This story later becomes a book and a TV movie.

1991

Ann and John Flavin of Arlington engage in what was then America's most expensive divorce, reportedly running up more than $10 million in attorneys' fees and other costs.

1992

Former attorney George Lott opens fire in the Fort Worth courtroom where his divorce was heard, killing two people and injuring three others. Tarrant County commissioners respond by ordering metal detectors installed in the courthouse.

Families First, a nationwide organization based in Atlanta, offers the first divorce recovery classes in Texas. At this writing, Families First classes are available in 14 Texas cities and classes through other groups are available in most jurisdictions.

1993

All family district court judges in Dallas County refuse to hold court until security measures are tightened after Hai Van Huynk, a 30-year-old machinist, shoots his wife in the hallway outside the family courts, then kills himself.

1995

The Texas Legislature passes an alimony statute.

1997

Jane Hopkins, a University Park mother, kills her children and herself after her divorce is final.

CHAPTER ELEVEN

Child Support

In Texas, child support is calculated by the Child Support Guidelines contained in the Texas Family Code. The charts that accompany the guidelines are updated each year. Under the Family Code, the court may order either or both parents to support a child until:

- The child is age 18 or graduates from high school, whichever happens later;
- The child is married or has his or her minority removed by law; or
- The child dies.

Under the court order, the parent who is required to pay child support is called the "obligor," while the parent who receives the support is the "obligee."

Child support is based on a formula that considers an obligor's net monthly resources, which consist of monthly gross wages minus taxes, union dues and health insurance costs. The formula is based solely on the resources of the obligor, and cannot include the re-sources of that person's spouse, if he or she has remarried.

Support Percentages

Once you calculate the net monthly resources, a certain per-centage of that net amount is payable as child support, depending on the number of children you are supporting. Those percentages are:

1 child	20% of obligor's net resources
2 children	25% of obligor's net resources
3 children	30% of obligor's net resources
4 children	35% of obligor's net resources
5 children	40% of obligor's net resources
6+ children	Not less than the amount for 5 children [10]

For example, say an employed person makes $3,600 per month in gross monthly wages and he has no other income. After taxes, union dues and health insurance expenses, the net monthly resources (income) is $2,718.89. Say this person has two children who receive child support. His child support payment would be 25% of net in-come, or $679.72 per month. These numbers would change slightly if the obligor has children from a previous marriage.

In most cases, this person would be obligated to provide the children with health insurance in addition to child support. This could be done directly through an employer, or through a separate policy. Health insurance can also be handled through the obligee's employ-ment, but the obligor would be responsible for any payment. And if this party chooses not to provide insurance, he is liable for any of the children's medical expenses.

If an obligor parent is self-employed, it may be difficult, if not impossible, to estimate the party's true income. Some self-employed people receive income in cash, and this income is difficult to prove in a contested divorce. If you are involved in a divorce with a self-employed person, financial records and other documentation are extremely important in proving your case for child support. Sometimes, the lawyer will look at consumption rather than income and illustrate to the court the purchases made by the spouse, despite the declared income.

Special Circumstances

Divorcing parties with high incomes and numerous assets, or those who share almost equal access to the children, follow rules that can be different from those described above.

If the obligor parent has more than $6,000 in net monthly resources, the first $6,000 goes into calculations for child support according to the guidelines. The court can then look at the income and assets of the parties and the needs of the child, to determine if additional child support should be paid.

Another common variable is the amount of possession or visitation allowed, especially in the case of parties having joint custody. If the mother and father have substantially equal assets and net resources and the children alternate living one week with one parent and one with the other, application of the child support guidelines may not be in order.

The Family Code specifically states that payment of child support should not be linked to how much visitation a parent receives. In other words, an obligee cannot deny visitation to an obligor parent because that parent is behind in child support payments. And an obligor cannot withhold child support due to visitation problems.

That's not to say these situations don't arise, through vindictiveness, petty behavior or ignorance of the law by some parents. But often they cause parties to risk contempt of court and can earn the offender a night or two in jail.

Child Support Collection

Child support is certainly the most overlooked and underpaid debt in our society. It is believed that people could get off welfare much easier if obligor parents simply paid their child support. All across the country, more than $34 billion in child support is owed from one parent to another. In Texas, $3.7 billion remains unpaid today. [11]

The Texas Attorney General's office is responsible for child support collections. Check the government listings in your telephone directory for the number of the nearest local office of the Attorney General. But there is much criticism of that agency's record. Many Texas lawmakers have talked about moving child support enforcement to another agency. You might also consult one of several private companies that will collect child support for you for a percentage of the money recovered. If you use one of these companies, make certain you pay no fees in advance. Check your Yellow Pages directory under "Child Support Collections" for a list of local companies.

The Family Code also provides for a local child support registry to receive court-ordered child support payments and forward them to obligee parents. Many counties in Texas use this kind of registry. Obligor parents pay a small fee to have a record made of their payments and to have checks forwarded. This method also provides evidence for court hearings when obligor parents fail to make payments as they were ordered.

Post-Majority College Support

In some states, you may receive child support beyond the age of majority for payment of specific college and other education-related expenses. In Texas, however, the payment of college expenses must be addressed in a divorce settlement and not by the court. Many settlement agreements specify that one parent will pay these expenses, or that the parties will divide them in some pro rata share. These expenses may include tuition, books and room and board. Other items such as a weekly allowance, fees, fraternity and sorority expenses and transportation to and from school also can be agreed to by the parties. But unless the parties agree to such a provision in the settlement agreement, the court cannot require a parent to pay for these items, since the age of majority (adulthood) in Texas is 18.

If, for example, a child wants to attend a private university, the agreement should specify the anticipated school and/or expenses to avoid any confusion in the future. Usually, scholarships are credited against these expenses. Child support does not continue after the child reaches 18 years of age, unless the parties make such support a part of the agreement.

CHAPTER TWELVE

Insurance and Taxes

David was being entirely too accommodating and Lauren didn't trust him. Each time they discussed something she wanted from the marriage, he said that he wanted her to have it. David wasn't known for his generosity, and so it was not until after the divorce was final, well into the next year, that she came to understand why he had been so nice about things. David was a certified public accountant, so he always filed their income tax forms. This year he knew something Lauren didn't know. They were due a large refund, and David would put the entire refund in his own pocket. David could afford to be generous.

Divorcing couples should address the issue of income tax liability in the settlement agreement. The parties cannot file a joint tax return for the year of the divorce. You should consult with an accountant about the tax consequences related to your divorce. If you do not have an accountant, your lawyer will suggest one who can evaluate the impact of your agreement from a tax standpoint.

Tax Liability or Refund

The previous year's tax liability or refund should be considered in any settlement agreement. Language should be added that specifies who is responsible for any deficiency assessment for liabilities for the prior tax year.

Many spouses are not aware of information contained in the tax returns. Usually they are surprised if a deficiency or audit arises after the divorce. In past years, spouses were required to satisfy tax liabilities caused by their exes, even if they knew nothing about the deficiency. Reforms of the Internal Revenue Service in 1998 exempted certain spouses from payment of tax bills due to the actions of an ex-spouse. Your attorney or accountant should be able to advise you on these matters.

Who receives the tax exemptions for the children is an important element of the settlement agreement. Generally, the primary custodial parent is automatically entitled to claim the income tax exemptions for any children. However, the parties may agree to divide or split the exemptions, due to other factors related to the settlement. For example, if one spouse is not working and has little income, tax exemptions may not help that spouse. The exemptions may benefit a spouse at a higher income much more than it might the spouse who is working for a minimal income. There is a level of income, though, where the higher wage-earner loses the benefit of any exemption for the children, based on the Internal Revenue code.

In the last few years, child support advocates have been outraged at so-called "deadbeat dads" who not only fail to pay what they owe, but also take the children as dependents on their taxes.

Internal Revenue Service Form 8332 is required to release the claim to the dependency exemption after the divorce. This form must be executed to satisfy the IRS concerning the exemptions in the future. You should consult with your lawyer and accountant in more detail concerning these issues to protect your interests.

Health Insurance for the Children

As stated before, the parent who is obligated to pay child support usually is required to provide and maintain hospital and major medical insurance for a minor child until that child reaches majority. If a child attends college, the coverage may be continued by agreement until the child graduates. In most cases, one spouse has health insurance coverage available through his or her employment. If that is not the case, usually the obligor parent must pay for health insurance separate from employment to cover the children.

Most often, spouses share the responsibility for any medical expenses not covered by the health insurance. These expenses include the deductible, reasonable charges for doctor, hospital, medical, prescription drug, optical, dental, orthodontic or other medically related expenses. This issue should not be taken lightly, because medical expenses associated with children can be monumental. In addition, if a child is diagnosed with a major illness such as leukemia, these expenses can be devastating and could lead to bankruptcy.

Health Insurance for the Spouse

Health insurance for a divorcing spouse can be a major issue in the settlement of a case. Generally, most health insurance plans will not allow you to continue to provide coverage for your ex-spouse.

Therefore, a spouse needing coverage has several options. First, you may obtain coverage through your employer. Often this is the cheapest solution to the problem.

Another option: a spouse may continue health insurance coverage for a limited time through the other spouse's insurance plan under the federal COBRA (Consolidated Omnibus Budget Reconciliation Act of 1985) plan or the Texas equivalent. Premiums associated with COBRA coverage usually are slightly higher than the previous payments through the employer, but the plan itself is administered through the employer and should offer all the benefits of the previous policy. Each spouse should confirm that this type of coverage is available before the final resolution of the case. The settlement agreement also should address who pays the premiums for this coverage.

Finally, the spouse can obtain coverage through an independent source. The settlement agreement can specify that the other spouse must pay the premiums for a specified period of time. This is a difficult provision to obtain from a judge in a divorce, however.

Pre-existing conditions may not be covered under the new insurance. If one spouse has a major health condition such as cancer or a heart condition, the condition may not be covered by the new insurance following the divorce. If this is a possibility, this issue should be very closely examined after the divorce in order to assess the costs associated with medical care. Medical conditions such as cancer and other major illnesses can play a large role in a party's financial need due to the costs associated with the illness as well as the limitations the illness may place on the spouse's ability to earn a living. As a result, health conditions may be a very disputed issue in your divorce, due to the potential implications. The husband of an ill wife may argue that she is not really sick, but simply making up an illness to get sympathy. To refute this claim, the wife's attorney may have to get a physician to testify to the wife's condition and its impact on her ability to work. Getting a doctor to testify in court is an expensive proposition. However, there may be a large amount of money at stake that would make such an investment worthwhile. The client may significantly reduce the cost by getting all medical records related to the condition for the lawyer to review. Otherwise, the lawyer will likely have to subpoena the medical records at considerable expense.

Life Insurance

If there are children involved and child support and other expenses are addressed in the settlement agreement, life insurance should be considered in the event the obligor spouse dies. Likewise, if financial payments are being made to the other spouse, the spouse making the payments should be required to maintain adequate insurance until there is no longer an obligation. It is a common practice that the obligor spouse be required to maintain specific life insurance policies of not less than a specified dollar amount, for a certain time period, and name the spouse or children as beneficiaries while there is a financial obligation under the divorce.

The settlement agreement should specify that the obligated spouse not modify the life insurance policies or diminish the value of the life insurance in any way, either by loan, pledge, assignment or reduction. Often, if children are involved, one spouse may require that a trust be established for the life insurance proceeds. Under such a trust, the obligor spouse specifies a trustee — often the former spouse or a family member — who is required to use the life insurance proceeds for the benefit of each child. When the children reach a specified age, such as 21, the trustee usually is required to distribute the entire remaining proceeds to them.

CHAPTER THIRTEEN

Who Gets the House?

The late redneck author and newspaper columnist Lewis Grizzard was fairly cynical about marriage after experiencing several of his own. One of his best-known lines was, "The next time I think about getting married, instead I'll just find a woman who hates me and buy her a house."

A house is the greatest investment most married couples will ever make. Often it is the most prized piece of property in the divorce, since usually it is the largest portion of the union's net worth and may also have much sentimental value.

Most people live in houses they can barely afford, with two people working and all of the family's effort on maintaining and paying for the home. Lending practices allow people to borrow an amount of money for a house that's just barely what they can pay back. Then the divorce takes place and these people are left trying to provide for two separate households along with child support payments. Sometimes the pressure gets to be too much and neither party is able to keep the house.

Is the House Really That Important?

When you consider whether the house is important enough to fight for, you will likely feel conflicting emotions. Some people believe they must get the house where their kids grew up and their lives were lived. Then they find their memories of life in the house are so bad that they don't actually want to live in it. And since they can't afford the payments, giving up their family residence is the best choice.

Carefully examine your financial condition before you decide what to do about your house. Look at your income plus the effect of child support or alimony payments, coupled with the debts each party will have to pay after the divorce. It is much better to realize ahead of time that you cannot afford the house than to fight for a house you cannot afford.

There are several ways to treat the residence, including the following:

- Keeping the house
- Selling the house
- Transferring the house to your spouse
- Transferring title, then selling it
- Deeding the house in exchange for a cash payment

Keeping the House

Either you or your spouse could wind up with total ownership of the house as part of the overall property settlement. You should take into consideration the true value of the residence, not just the "emotional" value. You may be unable to assess the true value of this property and may need to seek the advice of your accountant or a real estate professional.

Selling the House

If you and your spouse agree to sell the residence, the settlement agreement should provide that it will be sold with the proceeds divided as the parties have agreed. This agreement should deal with the tax consequences of the sale. One party may receive all of the equity or the parties may divide it in some other way, depending on the division of the other marital assets.

The property should be appraised before being placed on the market. If the parties cannot agree on an appraised value, one way to solve the dispute is for each party to select an appraiser to value the property. These two independent appraisers can then select a third appraiser who will set the value of the residence.

The parties should select a sales agent in the same way. If the parties cannot agree on a real estate agent, the parties can select different agents and the two agents can select a third person to serve as the agent for both parties. Until the real estate sells, the agreement also should specify who pays the mortgage payment, taxes, insurance and utilities. In addition, the agreement should specify that the party living in the home must provide routine maintenance and upkeep. The responsibility for paying the cost of reasonable and necessary repairs — structural, heating, cooling, roofing, and the like — also must be addressed.

The cost of necessary repairs or improvements to prepare the house for sale should be deducted from money received for the real estate, unless one of the parties agrees to bear this cost.

The agreement should specify that when the house is sold, the following items will be deducted from the gross sales price:

- The amount of the outstanding mortgage;
- The brokerage commission;
- Legal fees related to the sale;
- Cost of repairs or improvements;
- Cost of sale;
- Any other related terms of the settlement agreement, such as the payment of another debt.

Transferring the Residence To Your Spouse

If one party transfers interest to another, the agreement should specify that the transferring party conveys all interest in the residence. That party should also agree to execute a warranty or quit claim deed, whichever is proper for your case. The agreement should also specify who shall be responsible for the mortgage indebtedness. As with any transfer, the tax consequences related to the property should be addressed.

Transferring Title, Then Selling It

You can also specify in the settlement agreement that one party has use of the house for a specified period of time. When that time period expires, the house will be sold with the equity divided in a specified fashion. This option is common when there are young children and the immediate sale of the residence would be disruptive to their lives. Sometimes, one party is awarded the property for several months or years, often until the children graduate from high school or that party remarries.

The settlement agreement should specify how long the spouse can use the residence and what events are necessary to trigger a sale. The agreement must say who provides routine maintenance and up-keep and who pays the mortgage. If one spouse gets the house for a long period of time, the parties must decide whether the equity to be divided will be capped at a specified value or at the value at the time of sale. If you make all of the payments after the divorce, you will not likely want to share with your former spouse the appreciation in the residence that occurs after the divorce.

Deeding the House
In Exchange for a Cash Payment

Under this option, one party gets the house by paying the other party a cash sum. The terms of the payment must be addressed in the settlement agreement, along with payment of the mortgage obli-gation and all tax consequences of the transfer.

Impact of Keeping the Existing Mortgage

If the mortgage loan is a joint debt, both parties remain on the mortgage obligation unless the property is refinanced. Say your ex is responsible for the mortgage under the decree and he or she de-faults on it. In most cases, the mortgage company looks to you for payment of the debt if your ex cannot pay. Likewise, this mortgage obligation will show up on a credit report and will have to be addressed in future loan applications. This can sometimes be handled by showing the creditor a copy of the divorce decree that indicates you are not responsible for the mortgage obligation.

Failure of one party to pay the obligation can cause a lot of difficulty and may require court action to enforce payment of the mortgage or force the sale of the house. Proper documentation by your legal counsel can avoid some of the problems that result from a failure of one party to pay a mortgage under these circumstances.

In many cases, this problem cannot be avoided, especially if you cannot qualify for the mortgage alone and must sell the house anyway.

Tax Consequences

Often tax consequences associated with the sale of the house greatly affect the value of the award. For example, there may be capital gains taxes associated with the appreciation in equity in the residence over the original purchase price. Usually, you must transfer the equity to a new residence within 18 months to avoid additional tax consequences. You should meet with an accountant to analyze any potential tax liabilities associated with the residence before making a final determination of what to do with the property.

CHAPTER FOURTEEN

Dividing Major Assets

All assets of any real value must be covered in a settlement agreement. What "real" value means to you may not be the same to the other side, so the overall settlement must be weighed as a whole.

At issue are several classes of property: property that each spouse brought into the marriage; marital property acquired by both spouses during the marriage; gifts and inheritances received by both spouses during the marriage; and income received during the marriage. A multitude of potential assets will need to be addressed in the settlement agreement. In addition, liabilities or debts associated with these assets also must be addressed.

The assets in question may include the following:

- Furniture and furnishings of the residence
- Bank accounts
- Stocks
- Bonds
- Checking accounts

- Savings accounts
- Life insurance
- Retirement plans
- Individual retirement accounts (IRAs)
- 401(K) plans
- Stock options
- Business interests
- Patents
- Jewelry
- Automobiles
- Antiques
- Family heirlooms
- Sporting equipment
- Artworks
- China, silver and crystal
- Boats and trailers
- Personal collections such as coins and stamps
- Gun collections
- Business equipment
- Tools
- Yard equipment
- Whatever asset your spouse treasures

In an ideal situation, you and your spouse will be able to agree on most, if not all, of the property division. In that event, the settlement agreement needs to address the specific division of property and the responsibility of each party for any debts.

Personal Property

There are several ways to divide personal property, which can include household furniture and furnishings, goods, wares and appliances, along with each individual's clothing, jewelry and personal items. Typically, settlement agreements either specify that the parties have already divided the personal property and that neither party makes any claim to the other's property, or the agreement will contain a specific list of the property each party is to receive. If your relationship with your spouse is fairly amicable, you may be able to divide the household property on your own.

But I've seen people unable to agree on the simplest of issues, such as the division of towels and sheets. In this case, the agreement needs to specify every item each party receives. If the agreement states that you receive one-half of the pictures in the residence, it needs to specify exactly which pictures are yours. If you get into a fight over property, you may spend considerably more on legal fees to fight over a toaster or a couch than you would spend replacing that item. You must assess whether the emotional and financial cost of fighting over certain property is worth the end result. Many clients later claim that their decisions were based more on ego and pride than logic and that they did not even want the asset after they received it, due to the bad feelings associated with it.

Closely Held Businesses

If a business is involved in the divorce, the agreement needs to specify who receives the business and how it will be managed after the divorce. Usually, one party or the other gets total control over the business. But I've seen divorcing couples remain business partners. If one party is to receive the business, the agreement needs to specify if the other spouse is obligated for any debts or taxes, or if he or she receives any of the ongoing profits of the company. It also needs to specify who will pay any future debts and taxes associated with the business. If the company is successful, you will want an independent accounting of the books and records to determine its true value before finalizing the settlement.

More tricks are played around the value of a family business than almost any other asset of a marriage. It's an interesting principal that the party running the business during the pendency of a divorce seems to believe the company is worth so little. For example, a business owner might claim the last three years were the best years ever for the business, and that it is now likely to suffer a significant decrease in income just at the precise moment that the divorce is granted. An owner might claim that the market is way off and sales are suffering. This same business often begins to prosper again right after the divorce.

Businesses should be reviewed very closely due to the potential for managers to drastically affect the income figures during the divorce. I recall one example of a manager whose successful business was at issue in a hotly contested case. The owner claimed his company earned him only $20,000 in the previous year. We knew that the business had earned him much more than that in years past, sometimes as much as $250,000 a year before the divorce. Going on the assumption that this company was worth five times its annual earnings, we decided to believe the low-ball figures presented by the spouse/manager. We offered to purchase the business for $100,000 and guaranteed that we could have a cashier's check to him within three hours. We continued to increase our bid, but the manager would not sell even at twice that amount. The manager said there are a lot of factors that go into valuing a business and he felt it had potential. Of course, he had been practicing creative accounting. Once the manager refused to take the bait at twice the claimed value, we immediately began concentrating on the true value of the business. The overall settlement was much better for the wife of the manager because the business was worth a lot of money.

On the other hand, I've seen spouses who thought of the family business as some kind of fatted calf, since they had taken so much money out of it over the years. In several instances, managers eager to enhance their life-styles took huge salaries and bonuses each year instead of investing the money in up-to-date equipment and processes. That leaves the company an empty shell with little value as a marital asset.

Retirement Accounts

You may be entitled to a share of your spouse's retirement plan in a property division. This is a complex issue that must be addressed on a case-by-case basis. Retirement benefits may be one of the largest marital assets and should be considered before any determination is made on the fairness of the overall settlement agreement. In some lengthy marriages, one spouse may have a retirement plan valued at several times more than their home equity. Before the other spouse accepts the home in lieu of a share of the retirement plan, he or she should obtain a statement that shows the present value of the plan. If the account's value is not readily available, a lawyer can obtain the information necessary to value it from the account manager through the discovery process.

In addition, the survivor benefits under a retirement plan in the event of the spouse's death may also provide security and should be addressed in the settlement agreement. This agreement should prohibit benefits payable from being assigned or reduced in any fashion. If this is an issue in your divorce, spend some time verifying the value of the retirement plan and the tax implications.

Your lawyer needs to be well versed in the changes in the law concerning retirement plans and the use of a Qualified Domestic Relations Order (QDRO) to divide the plan. Under a QDRO, the plan can be split into two separate accounts to minimize the tax liability associated with dividing the plan prior to maturity.

CHAPTER FIFTEEN

Treasures Versus Junk

A good matrimonial lawyer will help you determine what the assets of the marriage are worth. Only you can determine which of those assets is worth a fight. In my experience, there are three major financial blunders made by most people in divorce:

- They forget that retirement accounts should be divided among the parties as part of a settlement;
- They fail to consider the debts in the marriage;
- They fail to place the correct value on closely held businesses.

There are many smaller blunders. For instance, most people forget that such assets as frequent flyer miles have value, and so they are not considered in the property settlement. I've seen studies which indicate that more than 80% of divorced people feel they were "taken to the cleaners" by their spouses in the divorce. This means one of two things; either 20% of the people have married many times and have amassed plenty of stuff from those marriages; or people tend to exaggerate and take the loss of assets very personally.

Other studies indicate that people feel most cheated when they lose the power to make the decisions concerning their property, such as when the court has to decide the property settlement between two divorcing people.

How the Court Divides Property

Since Texas is a community property state, all assets acquired during the marriage are owned equally by both parties. But the law does not specify that the division of community assets in a divorce has to be equal. If the parties cannot agree on a property division, the court will divide the community property after considering a variety of factors, including the following:

- Length of the marriage;
- The parties' respective ages, health, occupations, employability and ability to be trained;
- The earning capacity of the parties
- The degree to which a spouse has diminished his or her future earning capacity because of years spent caring for children;
- The opportunity for each spouse to acquire additional capital, assets or income in the future;
- The fault of the parties in the breakup of the marriage.

You Should Decide

It is in your best interest to work out an amicable division of personal property, instead of having a judge do it. For one thing, you know what you want, and you have a lot more time available to you than the judge does to go into painstaking detail. A judge doesn't really want to divide personal property. The judge will deal with the property division quickly, as part of the resolution of the entire case. The court doesn't have the time to ruminate over the fact that you are fond of that armoire in the bedroom, or that only you watched the big-screen television.

Often the judge will draw a big line somewhere down the list of property. He may split the property evenly, but that isn't guaranteed. If you don't get something you dearly want, it may be gone forever if your spouse does not want to trade it for something else of value. Even if you have to go to trial over more significant issues, try to work out the personal property issues with your spouse prior to trial.

Don't get caught up in an ego war over personal property. One custody case took several days in court and then the property issues were nearly resolved, except negotiations failed over possession of a Lincoln Towncar. Keep in mind, the custody issue was resolved, but issues remained concerning this automobile. When that type of situation happens, the parties' true priorities become very clear. The car ultimately was more important to the parties than their children.

CHAPTER SIXTEEN

Whose Debts Are Whose?

A commentator on the subject of divorce once said that fairness occurs only when you divide all the property among the parties, then throw the debts into the sea.

Payment of debts must be addressed in the settlement agreement, or this issue may come back to haunt you for years to come. The agreement should specify exactly which debts each party is responsible for after the divorce. For each debt, the responsible party should indemnify the other from any expense resulting from the indebtedness, including attorney's fees for enforcement of the indemnification. An indemnity is a promise to stand good for an obligation and to cover any expense incurred on the debt by the other party.

Which Debts Are We Talking About?

In the case of debts or assets, settlement agreements must state very specifically which ones are meant. Several years ago, I came across an agreement (which our firm had no role in drafting) that said "the parties have certain debts and the wife shall pay two of the debts and the husband shall pay two of the debts." Only it didn't specify which two debts each party was supposed to pay! An ambiguous agreement like this is impossible to enforce, because there is no way the court can interpret the specific debts from the vague terms.

Who's Liable for Debts?

A creditor may hold you liable if your spouse does not pay a debt incurred by both of you. The court has no authority to order a creditor or mortgage company to release one of its customers from liability. But if your spouse or ex-spouse does not make the payments as ordered, you can go to court on a contempt action. The creditor will still seek payment, but you might be able to secure a judgment or some recognition that the debt is not yours.

It is wise to pay off as many debts as possible, cancel the accounts or convert them into the name of one spouse during the divorce. You can also specify in the settlement agreement that certain debts be refinanced within a certain time to remove your obligation.

The court does not look favorably on a spouse who makes a large number of charges on joint credit cards immediately before separation or divorce. As a result, any recent charges need to be substantiated with receipts as being reasonable and appropriate.

Factors Considered in Apportioning Debts

The responsibility for marital debts is determined by a variety of factors including the following:

- Whose name the debt is in
- The purpose of the debt
- Who retains the asset related to the debt
- Financial resources of the parties
- Any agreement between the parties concerning the debts
- Overall apportionment of property in the agreement
- The length of the marriage
- The fault of the parties

You should provide your attorney with a list of the marital debts, including a breakdown of who incurred which debts. Clients also should provide a detailed list of purchases made to account for the debts, and the current status of those assets. This information should also include the name and address of creditors, as well as account numbers.

CHAPTER SEVENTEEN

Maintenance and Alimony

Let's burst the alimony bubble. The Texas Legislature passed an alimony statute in 1995, but it is written so narrowly that most people in this state would not qualify for alimony. Many people come into my office feeling that in the divorce they will get at least half of the community assets and then they will get alimony on top of that. This won't happen except in very rare instances, when the other side is represented by very poor counsel and the planets are in an odd alignment.

The Alimony Statute

The Texas Family Code says that spousal maintenance or alimony was intended as a temporary rehabilitative measure for a divorced spouse (usually the wife) who was a homemaker for many years and who lacks the job skills or the capital assets to support herself and her children.

In other words, alimony is considered a temporary measure to allow a woman to become trained to support herself. If you have no assets and no skills, and have been married at least 10 years, you can get alimony assessed for a period of three years, up to a maximum of $2,500 per month. The problem is that if you have any substantial assets, or receive them in the divorce, you won't qualify for alimony. And if your marital assets are limited and otherwise you qualify for alimony, the husband probably does not have the earning capacity to pay much, if any, of this support.

In this way, the alimony statute is more myth than reality, a way for lawmakers to satisfy women's rights advocates without actually changing anything. The alimony statute is relatively new and the courts are just beginning to give us some guidance in how the statute is to be applied.

The Alimony Reality

Poor women probably qualify for alimony more than any other socioeconomic group in Texas. But the people who actually receive alimony are mostly middle- and high-income people who agree in a settlement to accept contractual alimony payments rather than a lump-sum portion of the community assets.

Parties may want to pay alimony payments to their exes because they worry, for their children's sake, about that party's ability to handle a large chunk of money all at once. Often there are tax advantages to paying alimony, and the payor spouse will want to pocket the savings.

In the case of people whose only marital asset is a closely held business, the couple may agree to maintenance rather than having the business owner have to sell the company to give the other spouse his or her share of the equity.

If a spouse is going back to college to complete a degree or train for a job, the use of contractual alimony can allow the spouse to complete the schooling and thereby increase future earning capacity.

How the Court Decides

When alimony is assessed by the court, the following factors are considered in determining the nature, amount, duration and manner of periodic payments:

- Financial resources of the receiving spouse
- Education and employment skills of both spouses
- Length of the marriage
- Age, employment history, earning ability and physical and emotional condition of the receiving spouse
- Financial ability of the paying spouse
- Any financial mismanagement or concealment by spouses
- Contributions to education, training or increased earning power by one spouse to the other
- Property brought to the marriage by either spouse
- Contribution of a spouse as homemaker
- Any marital misconduct of the receiving spouse
- Efforts by the receiving spouse to pursue employment counseling

Temporary Maintenance

More common than alimony after a divorce is completed is a

temporary form of maintenance that is often awarded during the pendency of the divorce. Temporary maintenance is meant to pay for the transition from one household to another, and usually is paid to the spouse with the most limited resources and with temporary custody of the children.

CHAPTER EIGHTEEN

For Those Who Never Married

The virtual explosion of unwed live-in relationships over the past several decades has created a whole new body of law and problems as great as any experienced with conventional divorces. In 1986, there were four times as many unmarried couples living together as in 1970. In 1988, there were 2.6 million, up 63 percent from the number in 1980. And these numbers represent just those who were cohabitating at the time. In a random nationwide survey of 13,000 people, two University of Wisconsin sociologists found that 44 percent had lived with someone of the opposite sex before marriage. And 58 percent who were recently remarried had cohabited between marriages. [12]

Most couples who live together are in their 20s and 30s. Since many are the products of divorced parents, they shy away from marital commitments, with an eye toward testing out a live-in arrangement before jumping into marriage. It is ironic that the Wisconsin study indicates people who live together before marriage are more likely to divorce than those who don't.

How Legal Entanglements Happen

There is much to criticize about the system of marital dissolution in this country. But say what you will, it is far more organized, codified and, ultimately, civil than the mess that can take place when you have no legal paper between you as a guide in breaking up.

There is a laissez faire idea behind cohabitation. Man and woman meet. Man likes woman. Woman likes back. They spend some time together in one place of residence or the other. One gives the other a drawer for personal items, then the space grows to part of the closet. Without really planning it, they are living together. And since no planning went into the arrangement, rarely is any provision made for dissolution.

What happens if one party, who is paying one-half or more of the rent, decides to leave and the other party is unable to pay for the residence? The rules get even stickier if the couple buys furniture together, shares a bank account or has a child.

Common Law Marriage

In Texas, there really is no provision for the type of living arrangement described above. Texas is one of 11 states (and the District of Columbia) that recognize common law marriage. But in this state, common law is very nearly like conventional marriage. The requirements for a fully recognized common law union in Texas are as follows:

- The two parties must have agreed to be man and wife;
- They must live together as man and wife; and

- They must hold out to the public that they are married.[13]

The parties also may sign a declaration at the county clerk's office, attesting to the fact that they've entered into a common law marriage. However, a common law marriage is valid whether or not it is registered. The registration is helpful to eliminate the issue of whether the parties were actually married or merely living together.

Once established, a common law marriage has the same legal effect as conventional marriage. If couples do not go the common law route, live-in agreements are not part of family law, but are treated simply as contractual arrangements. To be legally binding, each party must provide something of value. For instance, both parties might contribute to the rent, while the man pays the utility bills in exchange for the woman cooking the meals. The two people must be dealing in good faith and the agreement cannot violate the law.

Palimony Doesn't Really Exist in Texas Law

In 1990, tennis star Martina Navratilova was sued in a Fort Worth court by her live-in lover, Judy Nelson, for violation of their "palimony" agreement. Although palimony doesn't exist as a legal principle in this state, Ms. Nelson and her attorney brought to court a videotape that showed Ms. Navratilova promising to love and care for Ms. Nelson. Ms. Nelson's attorney contended that the two women had made a binding contract. Ms. Navratilova's defense was simple: the "something of value" being provided by Ms. Nelson was sex. According to this interpretation, that amounted to prostitution and sex between two people of the same gender. Both are illegal under Texas law. The legal principles in this case were never tested in court, since the case was settled before it could get to trial.

But palimony has been tested numerous times — in both straight and gay relationships in Texas and around the country — by film actor Lee Marvin, Playboy founder Hugh Hefner, pianist Van Cliburn and others. Most palimony cases — especially those involving famous people — are settled out of court, since the threat of adverse publicity is more compelling than the legal principles involved.

Children of the Unwed

These situations naturally get more complicated when unmarried people have children. While a written agreement can settle where your new sofa will reside after a breakup, judges usually look at the best interest of the children in determining where *they* will live. As with children of conventional unions, custody does not always go to the mother. Fathers have gained custody in some instances, as have grandparents. The father is a "presumed father" and automatically has all the rights and duties of a parent if he consents in writing to be named on the child's birth certificate. Still, it's best to settle the custody question in a court order at the point of the breakup, so that it doesn't become an issue later in the child's life.

In 1986, more than one-fourth of the 14.8 million children in single parent households lived with a parent who had never married; and 800,000 kids were living with unmarried couples.[14] Many of these children are subjects of custody battles, conflicts over visitation rights and child support enforcement fights.

Proving Paternity is Essential

Statistics show over the years that children of unmarried unions receive far less child support, on average, than those from conventional marriages. In many cases, the fathers simply refuse to believe these are their children. Proving paternity is essential to getting child support in these instances. Several hundred thousand paternity cases are filed each year. The number is growing in part because of new, high-tech methods of establishing parentage. In years past, blood tests could be used to prove that a man was *not* the father, but these tests could not establish to a certainty that he *was* the father. Today though, DNA fingerprinting is being used to establish paternity to a 99% probability.

Men also use these tests to establish paternity and assert parental rights when the mothers fail to allow them to see and support children they believe are theirs.

CHAPTER NINETEEN

Evaluating Your Attorney

In the life of every contested divorce, there inevitably comes a time when the client asks, am I getting my money's worth from the attorney I chose?

Usually this evaluation stage is after the initial rush to gather information, after depositions and other discovery, maybe after the first settlement discussions, and usually before the case actually goes to trial. When you reach this point, emotions may be running high and you may not be thinking as straight as possible. At this time, you should evaluate your lawyer's performance by these benchmarks:

- Are you closer to resolving the divorce than you were when you hired your attorney?
- Do you feel that you'll get anywhere close to what was suggested you would get in the beginning, or have the attorney's promises gone by the wayside?
- Will you and your ex be able to deal with each other when the case is over?

- How much is the divorce costing you, and can you realistically say that you are going to come out with more than you are paying in attorney's fees?

Understand that lawyers are not magicians. They cannot perform miracles. If your spouse is a difficult person, higher fees and additional hassle are inevitable. If nothing is happening in the case, you should not expect daily updates. Relaying such information will use up your retainer needlessly. But when the action does commence, how does this person perform? Does he or she demonstrate knowledge, prepare well and come equipped with a plan?

If your objective in the beginning was to rev up a chainsaw and go after the opposition, don't be surprised if nothing is left — no relationships, no self-respect and no money. If you have decided that you and your attorney should follow a slash-and-burn policy, you are guaranteeing that you will not wind up with The Successful Divorce.

How to Pay Your Attorney

As stated before, you shouldn't expect your spouse to pay your attorney's fees as the case progresses, and most attorneys won't rely on that either, except in unusual circumstances. Family law has become a consumer area. Once attorneys controlled everything. Along with that was a gentleman's agreement concerning fees at the outset. This handshake concept was fairly common in business in earlier days. Just as cold cash upfront has taken the place of the handshake in other businesses, family law attorneys want to be paid in a timely manner.

I have seen one party to a divorce abscond with some piece of community property valuable enough to pay attorney's fees before the battle began. You need to know that the actions of both parties, even before the divorce is filed, are subject to the court's review. Most judges want to level the playing field. Each case is different, as are the feelings of each judge.

Most matrimonial attorneys take credit cards today. It is not uncommon for a spouse not to have access to cash, and so you might have to become creative in looking for the funds.

Could This Be
The Wrong Attorney for You?

Attorneys are not all the same. They don't all have the same temperament or work ethic. And if you aren't going to get along with your attorney in a divorce, you should know about it once the real work begins. I believe that the attorney's relationship with a client is like a hand and glove. If they don't fit each other, you should look for a better match.

The editor of The Successful Divorce series, Larry Upshaw, is a writer from Dallas who lectures attorneys on improving their public image. He says that all over the country, inattention to detail is the greatest problem clients have with their lawyers.

Your Attorney Doesn't
Return Phone Calls

Upshaw tells about two friends of his, one a divorce attorney and the other person needing a divorce, whom he brought together a couple of years ago.

They seemed to have compatible personalities, at least during the initial interview and the time when the divorce should have been filed. Then for months the attorney did not return repeated telephone calls from the client, who simply wanted to know about the progress of her case. Soon the client, who was in a panic, gave up expecting the attorney to call her back and began to ask for the legal assistant. The assistant continually referred her to the attorney, so the client was reduced to begging for news from the receptionist.

After more than six months had elapsed and the client had no notice that a divorce was filed, she sent faxes and then letters to the attorney. The situation caused her to become creative. Telling the receptionist that it was she, the client, who had failed to call back the attorney, she wrangled the attorney's car phone number out of the receptionist. After several tries, she got him en route.

Without skipping a beat, the attorney said things were beginning to happen and that he was on his way to the courthouse on some matter dealing with her divorce.

"And I've been meaning to call you because we have a settlement offer from the other side," said the attorney.

"What does it say?" asked the client.

"I don't know," replied the attorney. "I haven't read it."

This is not the type of communication that results in The Successful Divorce.

Too Active for Your Good

Sometimes an excited client can stir an attorney into too much action, resulting in a lot of wasted motion and money and, finally, an angry client.

Upshaw tells about a physician he knows who shopped around for "the meanest lawyer in town" to take on his soon-to-be ex-wife, whom he called a "crazy woman." When he found a divorce lawyer with the same glint of revenge in his eye, he paid the man a $10,000 retainer to begin a complex divorce with children and plenty of property involved.

Soon the "paper was flying" in the form of a divorce petition and numerous motions full of accusations about his wife and the mother of his children. When the doctor called the attorney's office, he was put through immediately. He would engage the attorney in long, rambling strategy conversations raging against his spouse. The attorney was even called by the doctor on the weekend, including calls to his cellular number and his lake house.

With all of that action, the doctor had to replenish the retainer with another $10,000, then $5,000 more. But things *were* starting to happen. Everything was in a complete state of upheaval. His in-laws, who were close to him before all of this, were furious with him. And his children were so upset that he had to pay for their counseling. The doctor's practice began to suffer an unusual number of appointment cancellations, and the level of tension was so high that he had trouble sleeping.

Soon the doctor/client had enough. When he called to complain, the attorney reminded him that he said to "spare no expense," " be aggressive" and "make the other side miserable."

"But I also said to win," said the client. "I've spent $25,000 and I'm farther away from winning than I was when I started."

This client eventually learned the hard way about winning at "all cost." He sat down with the attorney, and they began to handle the case in a more constructive fashion. Once the tensions calmed, the parties were able to settle the case. The moral of this story is that you should not set out to destroy the other side. That's destructive enough when it's your idea. If it's your attorney's idea, hold on to your wallet. I always tell clients that I won't tell them how to do their job as long as they won't tell me how to practice law. While it's true that you are the boss of your case, your attorney is the professional. You should not pay for his services if you aren't going to listen.

What is communicated in your first meeting with a client should be examined a little later in the case. Often people mature during the course of a divorce once they get past some of the emotion. It is the lawyer's responsibility to inform clients of what is reasonable. It is the responsibility of clients to hear what is being told them, and to heed that advice.

Legal Eagle, Fly Away

Most disputes between attorneys and clients can be settled with meaningful communication. But if it becomes apparent that the lawyer is not making as much progress as you would like, you may have to consider seeking new counsel. This is a drastic move, one you should make only after asking yourself if you are doing this because you aren't making progress, or because this attorney won't accede to your unrealistic demands?

You could be like a person who smokes three packs of cigarettes a day firing doctors until you find one who says it's okay to smoke. That doesn't mean it's okay to smoke. It only means that you've found a doctor who says it's okay. You'll still die of lung cancer, but you'll die with your doctor's permission.

It can be expensive, both in money and your ability to move

your divorce along, to constantly change attorneys. Changing attorneys without a good reason usually means the client is the difficult person, not the lawyer. When a series of lawyers tells you that what you want is unattainable under Texas law, you may consider that *you're* doing things wrong.

But if you have made up your mind to actually change attorneys, the process should not be difficult. Simply call or write your lawyer and ask to have your file sent to you or to another attorney you have retained. If you cannot reach your attorney by phone, send a fax or letter and call the office to confirm that it was received. For the good of your case, the timing of the change is important. Making a change when you are facing an immediate court appearance can hurt your case and cause your new attorney to begin work well behind the opposition.

Whenever you terminate an attorney, you should receive a refund of any retainer amount being held by the retiring attorney, or pay an existing balance due, subject to the terms of your written fee agreement.

The bottom line is that this is *your* divorce, hopefully the only one you are ever going to get. You are entitled to be represented by legal counsel you respect and can communicate with; one whose representation will allow you to sleep at night, hopefully without a sleeping pill.

Some Say He's Good, Others Lucky

"As a young lawyer, I took on a woman's contested divorce case, with property and child custody at issue, on Friday prior to a Monday trial setting. But a stroke of luck saved me. The husband was set for a criminal trial the same day, and so our trial was postponed for six weeks.

"It seems the man and his children were Christmas shopping when another driver cut them off on the expressway. The husband, a powerful guy at about 240 pounds, followed the other car into a shopping mall parking lot, pulled the teenaged driver (about 100 pounds lighter) out of his car and screamed profanities at him. Then, in view of several thousand holiday shoppers, he pressed a snub nosed .357 revolver against the catatonic teen's head and threatened to blow his brains out.

"Despite eyewitness reports and other evidence, the husband took the stand and steadfastly claimed 'mistaken identity.' He was shocked when the jury returned a guilty verdict after 45 minutes. In the trial's punishment phase, the husband took the stand again and wept bitterly, admitting his crime but saying alcohol made him do it. When the husband finished his amazing statement, the judge excused the jury, had the husband arrested and charged with aggravated perjury and continued the trial.

"Even more amazing, the husband insisted on going through with our trial. I subpoenaed the judge in the criminal trial and had him recite the husband's statements and the incredible result. My client won her custody case, thanks to my intuitive ability to take advantage of the 'lucky break' provided by her husband."

Rick Robertson
McKinney

Part Four
Going to Court

CHAPTER TWENTY

Our Court System

Divorces in Texas are heard through the system of state district courts (and some county courts at law) presided over by judges elected by the people of that jurisdiction.

Family Courts, District Courts

In the large cities, certain district courts handle only domestic relations cases, including divorces and child custody matters. The judges of these courts are often board certified family law specialists, and they deal exclusively with family issues. These courts are different from juvenile courts, which deal mostly with matters relating to minors, often in the criminal arena.

In Dallas County, for instance, there are seven family district courts that handle divorce matters. Tarrant County (Fort Worth) has six such courts, while Harris County (Houston) has nine of them. In these counties, each family district court also has an associate judge assigned to hear temporary and other matters.

In the counties of Bexar (San Antonio) and Travis (Austin), divorce cases are heard by civil district courts and are not handled by specialty courts. Galveston, Longview, Midland and El Paso each have one court that is specifically designated a family district court. District judges in the remaining counties hear all kinds of civil matters, from business lawsuits to divorce.

Because of the difference in the way cases are heard in various settings, court procedures (and the justice dispensed by these courts) can mean something different in Marfa from what they mean in Dallas or Houston. It always helps to know something about the judges and the workings of the court in the jurisdiction where your case is heard. Even if you decide to import a big city family law specialist to handle your divorce in a rural county, it is usually helpful to have local counsel who can advise you in dealing with a particular court.

Temporary Hearings

Setting the ground rules in a case is an important first step in the divorce process. From the time the divorce is filed, you and your spouse must decide where the children will live, who will live in the house, how much child support or spousal support will be paid and what will happen to certain assets and bills before the divorce is final.

In most instances, these issues can be settled between the parties or their lawyers. A phone call or two should be enough to put the process in motion. I've seen parties become very creative at this time. For instance, if they couldn't decide who would stay in the home, I've seen people agree that the children would stay in the home and each parent would alternate weeks living with them. This does not work in many cases, but who's to say it will never work.

Only in the most contested of cases should you have to resort to a temporary hearing to resolve these matters. These hearings usually are held within 14 days after the divorce is filed. Temporary hearings are expensive and time consuming, but may be necessary if the parties simply cannot agree. In the Texas counties that have specialty courts, most divorce-related pretrial activities are handled by associate judges. These associates are appointed magistrates who assist the family court judges. In the jurisdictions that don't employ associate judges, temporary issues are decided by the judges themselves.

Judge or Jury?

In many contested divorces, the big question is whether you allow a judge to decide your fate or ask for a jury trial. This state has a long tradition of allowing people their day in court before a jury of their peers. Texas is the only state that extends this right to child custody issues.

If you and your spouse cannot decide the value of that beautiful 14th century French armoire you hang your suit in each day, it is your right to have a jury decide the issue. Of course, jury trials generally take longer and cost more than having a judge hear the case. So you might wind up paying more than the armoire is worth to decide its value.

The ideal situation is for you and your former honey to agree, even grudgingly, on all the important matters in a divorce. But failing that, judges can make most of the decisions involving property.

Where juries have been important historically is in deciding child custody issues. Sometimes a case might not be so strong on the finer points of the law, but there exists a powerful emotional context. You may want your decision in the hands of everyday parents and grandparents, who aren't judges and whose grasp of the law isn't as great as that of a judge. But the fact that these everyday folks might know a loving, caring relationship when they see it, and don't deal each and every day with the difficulties of such legal disputes, may make them ideal to hear your case.

Under Texas law, it is the judges who decide on the division of property when the parties are unable to forge and agreement. They also have the final say on access to children as well as the rights and duties parents shall have with respect to the children after the divorce.

You cannot be expected to make the decision of whether a jury should be used in your case. That decision is a complicated one you need to discuss carefully with your attorney. If your lawyer has never tried a divorce case before a jury, don't be surprised if his or her first inclination is not to use a jury. You are entitled to know what factors your attorney is considering in the decision and you should insist on being a full participant in this process.

CHAPTER TWENTY-ONE

Preparing for Trial

In divorce, as with most things in life, those who come to court the most prepared have a better chance of winning. This principal extends from the preparation of witnesses and your theory of the case to the way you look and act on that important day.

Once your attorney becomes familiar with your rendition of the case, all the financial information, possible depositions of available witnesses and anything else relevant to the case, it is important to review the entire case prior to trial.

Each hearing affects the eventual outcome of your case. You and your lawyer should meet to discuss the preparations. You should be told what will happen in the hearing and have the relevant issues that need to be addressed by your side explained to you. Your counsel may even request that you attend a trial similar to yours so that you can get a good idea of the intensity of the proceeding and what to expect from the opposing counsel and the judge.

In many cases, your lawyer will prepare you for the hearing by running through questions that might be asked in court and those the opposing counsel might ask you. Probably more important than what you will be asked is how you will answer. Of course, you always tell the truth. A reputable family law specialist would never ask you to get on the stand and lie. But there are many ways to answer the same question, and you must rely on the experience of the attorney to let you know the proper way to reply.

For example, a client of mine had a family history of high blood pressure. Recently, he had been prescribed blood pressure medicine by his doctor. He expected his wife's attorney to attempt to portray him as a sickly individual unable to care for their young son. In truth, many people in his family had died of heart attacks. But although he had speculated on the possibility of heart trouble for himself, he had never been diagnosed with a heart condition and was a healthy man in his mid-30s.

To the question "Do you take blood pressure medicine?" the answer was "yes." To the question, "Do you have heart disease?" the answer was an emphatic "no." If the attorney wanted to delve into his family history, perhaps he could establish some tenuous link between this man and the fate of his ancestors.

Perhaps through picking nits you could suggest something awful that might happen some decades in the future. But without evidence to the contrary, this man was healthy. To the jury, it seemed like a needless invasion of his privacy. To the judge, it was simply a waste of time.

Sifting the Ingredients of a Marriage

Knowing how much or how little information a judge or jury needs to make a decision is the art of being a family law specialist.

Many clients want to regale the judge or jury with minute details of the marriage. A good lawyer is keenly aware of the limited time and the possibility that the judge will become frustrated or the jury bored if overwhelmed with irrelevant or repetitive details.

Think of your lawyer as a chef working over a giant pot into which he pours, sifts and grates all the ingredients, herbs and spices necessary to make the soup that is your marriage. It's your lawyer's job to combine the correct ingredients in just the right combination to make the soup taste just right to the finders of fact. Too much of even the best ingredients and you have a bad bowl of soup.

Once you have established that your spouse abused your children, move on. If the lawyer wastes too much time listing the same facts over and over again, the judge may turn the disgust he might feel with your spouse into anger with the party who is wasting the court's time. Don't give the opposing party an opportunity for rehabilitation in the eyes of the court, no matter how eager you are to tell the whole sad story.

The time you spend on the witness stand answering questions from your attorney is when you establish your side of the case. If the other side is asking you questions, this cross examination usually is limited and controlled by the other side. Most of the questions you are asked will be "yes or no" questions, and that's all you will be allowed to say. You may want to answer, "Yes, but that is because he ...," and the other lawyer will cut you off. That lawyer may ask, "Have you ever yelled at your children?" Most likely, the answer is "yes," but you will have an uncontrollable urge to elaborate. Most clients become frustrated when the lawyer on the other side stops them, saying, "Please, just answer the question yes or no." Sometimes the strategy of the other side is to purposely frustrate you, so you will lose your temper and show the judge or jury what a difficult person you are.

I've seen this work with the most genteel people, who suddenly lose control of the situation. The best family law specialist will practice with you, asking all those questions in the safety and comfort of the law office. In this way, the attorney plays devil's advocate until you react as you should. Remember, it's not necessarily what you say, but how you say it, that is most important.

Get Friends, Family to Court

One of the most distasteful aspects of a divorce trial is the need to persuade friends and family members to testify on your behalf. While you can say all kinds of nice things about yourself, judges and juries tend to believe others saying the same things about you. The theory is that you must be a good person if people will take the time and risk alienating your spouse to make a point in your favor.

Sometimes these people are the only ones who can corroborate certain claims, such as physical abuse or a gambling addiction.

You never know how people will do on the stand until you speak with them in person. I remember years ago interviewing the neighbor and landlord of a client in a child custody case. All I hoped to establish with this man was that my client paid his rent on time and could be seen playing in the front yard with his son. It was really just one more character reference for a man who had many. As I questioned the neighbor, I could see the distress on his face. I asked what was the matter and he burst out, "But what if they find out about *my* kids?" It seems that decades ago, in a land far away, he had abandoned his own family and hadn't seen his children since. Of course, the other side wouldn't spend the money researching the past life of such a relatively unimportant witness. The only way they would know his story was if he blurted it out on the stand. His secret was safe with me as I struck him from my witness list.

Work with your attorney to decide who will testify for you and what questions they will be asked. Rely on the expertise of your attorney to figure out who will help you and who is extraneous to your case.

You may not like having to ask a person to come to court for you, especially when he or she knows the other side and would risk losing a friendship over the testimony. But if your attorney says that person is essential to your case, it's your job to persuade your friend to testify. Failing to act on this need could endanger your claim in court.

Get Plenty of Rest

Nothing can bring on sleepless nights like a contested divorce case, especially when child custody is at issue. It is important that you come fully prepared, remembering what your attorney told you and what certain witnesses will say. It's also important that you come to court rested and ready for the fight.

Try to take your mind off the proceedings the night before. Go to a movie or take in a sporting event. Don't succumb to pressure. No matter what happens in court, your life will go on. And if you walk into court rested and refreshed, things always go better than you think they will.

CHAPTER TWENTY-TWO

Your Day in Court

The young wife and mother was running late for court. As she circled the courthouse, looking for a parking space, she glanced nervously at her watch.

Up in front of her, a large sedan pulled out from a side street. At the wheel was a bald man so short that he looked through the steering wheel as the traffic whizzed by him. The young mother was behind him now. He was taking his own sweet time and as she followed behind him it drove her crazy.

Just then, the woman saw a car pulling out of a parking space on the street. Her tires screeched as she pulled around the short man in the big car and squeezed past. He was not paying close attention, but she could see him react. She pulled headfirst into the parking space, so the short man couldn't beat her to it. He drove by her, shaking his fist and muttering something she could not make out.

It was only five minutes until her divorce trial was set to start. At stake was several million dollars in property, along with the future of her two children.

She took time to compose herself in the hallway outside the courtroom. They would select a jury this morning, and she had to be sharp. It was important that she be at her best in front of these people, to make a good impression on them and win them over to her view of this marriage.

She walked into the courtroom head down, her eyes glued to the floor. She smiled faintly at her lawyer and his legal assistant as she pulled out the chair, sat down and looked up.

Already seated on the front row, near the end, was a particularly noticeable prospective juror — the short bald man from the large car.

How to Present Yourself

From the moment you leave your home, you are part of the court system and should be careful how you act. As the woman discovered in the example above, you never know who you'll run into or how that person will react to you. For any court appearance, clients should dress professionally. For men, I generally recommend a suit or nice pair of slacks, a white shirt and a tie. A nice dress or suit is appropriate for a woman. If you have any questions about your wardrobe choices, be sure to ask your lawyer for suggestions. First impressions are important in all aspects of life, but they are most important in a custody or marital dispute where a judge or jury is forced to evaluate the credibility of the parties in a short time.

As a very young attorney, I thought my clients could figure out for themselves how to dress appropriately for court. I handled a case early in my career where it was important for my client to dress conservatively as a counterpoint to the wild look of her playboy husband. I assumed after we talked that she would show up for court as I had envisioned. When she arrived, she was wearing a short skirt and flashy jewelry. She looked like she was going dancing right after our court session. I quickly asked for a delay to rectify the problem. Never again would I leave such a detail to chance.

Those appearing in court should always act in a mature and professional manner, never threatening. In the past few years, there have been numerous incidents of threats or actual harm done to one party in a divorce by the other. Judges who've seen this have become increasingly sensitive to any hint of violence, and they will jail the potential offender, if necessary.

Always be calm and cool, even though deep down you may be quite the opposite. Many cases have been settled because a client came to court poker faced, convincing the other side he or she was not concerned about going to trial.

Assuming you are unable to settle your case, eventually it will be set for trial on the court's calendar. It is said that one-half of all cases filed in the courts of Texas involve some facet of family law. That's a lot of cases to demand time on the calendar. The first case setting usually is three months or more after the filing of the divorce petition. It is not uncommon for a case to be reset several times before it actually reaches trial. Continuances occur for a variety of reasons: the parties' readiness to try the case; conflicts in the attorneys' schedules; conflicts in the client's schedule; and conflicts in the court's docket. If the judge is already in trial on another case or has an immediate issue to address or an older case to hear, your case may be passed over and continued to a later date.

A spouse who will owe money to the other spouse after the divorce often tries to continue the case as long as possible. This either

avoids imposing a premature obligation on the client or forces a settlement in the case. Over time, many people become anxious to settle
— even to the point of accepting an inadequate settlement offer —
because they've waited so long for their money. Once you realize
that a settlement cannot be reached, it may be a long time before the
case actually goes to trial. The delay needs to be factored into any
decisions surrounding the settlement of the case and whether the
expenses associated with the delay will be outweighed by the trial
court's potential ruling.

Your spouse may not believe you will actually go to trial. This
is especially true if your spouse was the dominant person in the marriage. In such cases, it is often beneficial for you to follow through
with the drama and theatrics of a trial. Otherwise, your spouse will
continue to harass you after the divorce, believing he or she can get
away with it.

Definitely Scheduled For a Hearing ... Maybe

For most people, the courthouse is an eye-opening experience
that bears no resemblance to the courthouse on your television set
or movie screen. Because 10 to 15 cases may be set on the judge's
docket the same day as your case, the parties and witnesses for each
case on the docket fill the courtroom. The hallways outside the courtroom are often lined with hard wooden benches filled to capacity
with more parties, witnesses and lawyers trying to resolve their cases
at the last possible moment.

Usually, the judge calls the docket first thing in the morning
and checks the status of each case with the attorneys representing

the parties. The attorneys may request an opportunity to talk settlement with each other. They may request a continuance or ask to speak with the judge about a particular issue that needs clarification before the case can proceed. If the parties are ready for trial, the judge will determine, based on all of the cases set that day, which one will be heard.

The judge's determination is based on a variety of factors. First, the case with the oldest filing date usually has priority. Sometimes, the judge looks at the seriousness of the issues at hand. If there is an emergency issue on the docket — such as an immediate threat of abuse or theft of property — the court usually attempts to resolve this issue, even if it is only a short-term fix.

When several emergencies are set on the court's docket the same day as your case, the judge picks the most immediate emergency and one the court has time to handle. If the judge is already in trial on a case from the previous day, it is normal to proceed with that case and reschedule all the others. This is how the judicial system works, and your lawyer can't do much about it. Even though you waited three months to get to trial, you prepared for the trial with your lawyer and your witnesses are all present at the courthouse, your case may be continued over your lawyer's objections.

If witnesses must come from far away or other hardships make it difficult for a party to come to court, your lawyer may be able to call the courthouse on the day before your case is set to determine where you are on the docket and what kind of cases are set before yours. This tells you to some degree whether your case is likely to go to trial. Some judges will tell the lawyer who is calling that a trial is in progress or a more pressing case must be resolved. Other judges require you and your lawyer to be at the courthouse every time the case is set. If your lawyer is an expert in this area, he should be able to tell you whether the judge and his office can help coordinate the scheduling of the trial.

Keep Your Cool in Court

During any court appearance, remain focused on the issue at hand. Sit up straight in your seat, speak clearly and be polite. Remember that the judge is evaluating your responses and your overall personality to determine whether you are the evil person the other party says you are. Do not be argumentative or hostile with the other side or answer questions in a haughty or sarcastic fashion.

Your lawyer is the one to handle the relevant arguments, not you. The talented trial lawyer on the other side will want to get you upset on the stand so you will lose your temper and show the judge the evil personality that the other side has described. Human nature makes us all want to respond when attacked by another person. Keep in mind that the other side's goal is to get you into an argument and affect your focus during the trial. Do not help them achieve their goal.

Briefly Tell the Truth

When you are questioned by the other side, give truthful and accurate answers. Besides the fact that lying on the stand is unethical and illegal, it may ruin your credibility in front of the trial judge if the other side can discredit your testimony. Often you expect questions about factors that led to the breakup of the marriage. Discuss with your lawyer ahead of time how to handle these issues at trial.

Do not offer more information than the other side has requested.

It is not your job to prove the other side's case. If the lawyer does not ask the appropriate questions, you may not have to provide certain information. This principle applies to every question you are asked. Once you have answered the question as briefly as possible, be quiet. If you have concerns about how to answer certain questions, you need to discuss these concerns with your lawyer beforehand.

Your lawyer will go over a specific plan for handling the case at trial, based on the information available and how he knows the judge in that particular court will respond to certain information. Even though you may think a fact or piece of evidence is absolutely imperative to clear your good name, it may annoy the judge and throw your lawyer off. Most divorce lawyers want to know exactly what you plan to say when you are on the stand. Your refusal to follow your lawyer's advice may cause you to lose your case.

Most people don't try to tell their dentist how to drill their teeth. But for some reason, giving instructions on how to try a lawsuit is a common trait with many clients. If you feel your attorney needs your guidance in how to handle matters in court, perhaps you need to look for new counsel.

The Final Decree of Divorce

When the divorce is resolved, the judge will sign a document called a final decree of divorce. This document divorces the parties and spells out the terms and conditions of the divorce. If the case is settled, the final decree of divorce usually contains a settlement agreement signed by the parties and makes it binding on both parties. If the case is tried in court, the decree spells out the court's ruling concerning the trial.

It is important that you read and understand all the terms and conditions of the decree and any settlement agreement, since you can be held in contempt for not abiding by the terms of the order. If you have questions or concerns, your lawyer needs to explain your rights and responsibilities. Emotions are at a high level during a trial or during the settlement of the case. It is normal for people to forget certain issues, such as the exact property distribution from the marital residence. You should also put the final decree of divorce in a place for safekeeping, since you will likely refer to it in the future as disputes or questions arise about the divorce.

Our Marriage, Just As I Pictured It

"Several years ago I had this client, a man, who was awarded a number of pieces of furniture from the marital residence in the final decree of divorce. The case had been particularly bitter and my client had been accused of a number of things, including that he was obsessive and picky in the way he did things.

"When he went to pick up the furniture, which including many valuable antiques, he brought along an off-duty policeman. He also brought a camera and took individual photos of each piece. To the casual observer, it was yet another example of his offensively detailed behavior. The husband figured, correctly so, that his wife would substitute cheap imitations for some of the most valuable antiques he was awarded in court.

"The man had, of course, taken photos of the real antiques at an earlier time. With the policeman as our witness, we were successful with a contempt action against the wife. The very behavior that she complained about got the best of her in the end."

Ike Vanden Eykel

Part Five
Once Your Divorce Is Final

CHAPTER TWENTY-THREE

Appealing Your One Best Shot

You've had your day in court. This was your one big attempt to show that you deserve to run the family business or guide the lives of your children. In most cases, this is your one time inside a domestic relations court. Overturning the trial court's decision in a divorce case is difficult and rare. That's why it is so important to prepare your case well and get what you need either through settlement or trial. Still, there are two main avenues available for post-judgment review and relief — a motion for a new trial and an appeal to a higher court.

Motion to Set Aside Or for a New Trial

Either party has the right to file a motion to set aside the decree or request a new trial if you are not satisfied with the court's ruling. Under Texas law, this type of motion generally must be filed within 30 days of the date of the court order.

In reality, a motion like this usually is not successful unless the court failed to consider a material fact in evidence or the court made a clear and distinct error in its ruling. The trial judge heard your entire case. He is familiar with it and can review his notes to determine if an error occurred. With a motion for a new trial, you are asking the trial judge to admit that a mistake was made and correct it. If this type of motion is not successful, you are then forced to use the appeal process to change the decree.

Time Limits for Appeal

Either party has the right to appeal a final decree of divorce. From the trial court, you must appeal to the Texas Court of Appeals. There are 14 such courts located in various cities around the state. Each Court of Appeals has up to 13 judges. A three-judge panel from one of these courts would hear your appeal.

If you are not satisfied with the action of the appeals court, you can apply to the Texas Supreme Court to review your case. Unlike an appeal to the Court of Appeals, you do not have the absolute right to appeal a case to the Supreme Court in Texas. That court decides which cases it will hear. Appealing a divorce case all the way to the Texas Supreme Court is rare and expensive and can be very complicated.

Last-Ditch Effort

An appeal is a last-ditch effort to change the divorce decree, and often an appeal will fail. The law is specific as to which issues can and cannot be appealed, and the standard of review for such an appeal is stringent. Most successful appeals of divorce cases deal with specific issues like a trial judge not allowing the testimony of a witness who is very important to the case.

An appeal is an expensive legal procedure that can cost far more than the divorce process itself. The lawyer must write a history of the case for the Court of Appeals. If you hire a different lawyer to handle the appeal, that lawyer will have to spend many hours getting familiar with the facts of the case before anyone can write the appeal. If the appeal is not successful and the matter is then appealed to the Supreme Court, the lawyer may have to draft additional documents and that means more expense.

So you see, it is much more effective and efficient to handle the case properly at trial. Relying on the appeal process to remedy an injustice that occurred at trial is possible, but it's a long shot at best.

CHAPTER TWENTY-FOUR

Enforcing Your Decree

The Maisal family operated like many traditional ones. Whatever Melvin Maisal said was law. He was the provider, the husband and father, and he called the shots. His wife, Karen, stayed at home, took care of the children and assisted in his climb up the corporate ladder. But one wrinkle of modern life crept into this family's life. Melvin wanted a divorce, and he wanted it on his terms.

There was confusion and a lot of doubt on Karen's part, but she made her way through to a settlement that everyone considered generous. She would never be forced into the working world, and the lives of her children would continue as nearly normal as possible.

Since the divorce was Melvin's idea, he felt obligated to give her the house and plenty of money. He also gave her complete authority over the children. He figured that he would have to step in and tell her what to do anyway. That was the pattern of their marriage, as he saw it. There was no reason to believe that would change.

At first, Karen went along with whatever her ex-husband wanted. After all, most of the decisions she made for her family dealt with such issues as what brand of spinach to buy. As time passed, though, and she became more independent, Karen became accustomed to providing answers to the larger questions of their lives. Soon she wanted to move to another part of the city. This required that the children change schools. Melvin objected violently to her choices. How dare she make a decision on her own? And what's this non-sense about asking him why he was objecting?

Thus began a pattern of bullying, then standing up to the bully, that lasted for years.

Flexible or by the Book

Only the two parties to a divorce can determine whether they consider the decree set in stone or simply a guideline for looking at their everyday life as people change and their children make their way to adulthood.

If you have an ex who continually suggests changes to the daily routine, you need to ask yourself the following:

- Is this change better for the children?
- Can it bother or hurt me? Is it a short-term benefit, but a long-term problem?
- If I agree to this now, will it become the basis for some later change that I don't want?
- Can I trust this person to do this unofficially, or do we need to do it legally?

There are no hard and fast rules to determine how much you give and when you say that's enough. Only common sense can provide the correct answers. I've known divorced couples whose actual lives bore little resemblance to the divorce decree after several years.

No one ever believes their children actually will grow up and things will change. A story on the aftereffects of a child custody case in *D Magazine*, the city magazine of Dallas, summed it up best:

> "In our case, a cute little white-haired preschooler would grow into a 6-foot-tall, 210-pound mountain of hormones, complete with car keys, girlfriends and responsibilities. And parents who divorced each other long ago would find that, like it or not, they still had a relationship.
>
> "Only in a few very extreme cases does the 'losing' parent just go away and leave the children's welfare to the former partner. The vast majority of cases, however bitterly contested, involve two dedicated parents who settle into a awkward détente — not really together, not really apart." [12]

Most people who successfully deal with a divorce make lots of changes as the kids grow up and mature. These are people who act in the best interest of their children, have few clashes of random ego and who truly want the best situation possible for everyone involved. So there is hope. It just takes time for the healing to take place.

On the other hand, there are those parents who are driven nearly insane because the ex-spouse was supposed to have the children back home at 8 p.m. and here it's 8:15 and they aren't home. Only in the most extreme cases, where child abuse is suspected or kidnapping a possibility, is this acute emotional investment warranted.

Your Annual Legal Checkup

Hopefully, you will only need one divorce lawyer in your life. Even so, I look at those people I help through a divorce and its aftermath as clients forever. At the beginning of the process, I refer clients to the advisers they need to get their lives back in order. These professionals may be CPAs, financial planners, bankers, even housecleaning or babysitting services. Then at the end of the divorce, I usually suggest that when the need arises, the client should come into my office, update me on his or her life and the lives of the children, how the visitation schedule is working, whether child support is being paid on time and generally how things have been going.

At these legal help sessions, clients get an opportunity to ask a variety of questions, such as:

- My ex just got a better job. Can we get more child support?
- My ex wanted nothing to do with the children after the divorce. Now he wants visitation. What should I do?
- My ex's parents want to visit the kids, but I don't want them in my house. Any suggestions?
- I have a chance to help my career by moving to Los Angeles, away from my kids. How can I maintain contact?
- I am thinking about remarrying. What are the ramifications?
- I believe my ex hid some assets at the time of the divorce. Can we go back to court to recover them?

Just like you should have a physical examination and tune up your car on a regular basis, you should have a professional check out your legal well-being on a regular basis, especially if you have children or continuing financial ties to your ex.

Sessions like these have allowed me to help clients get increased child support payments, recommend a mental health professional for a child in trouble or suggest an attorney in another field to handle an unrelated legal matter that a client was having trouble resolving.

Pigs Get Fat, Hogs Get Slaughtered

The old idea that in a divorce, you must give no quarter, allow nothing but what you absolutely must and stick strictly to your guns may win respect from your buddies and it certainly looks good in the movies. It does nothing for you in the family court system. If you can afford to be generous with your ex (and especially your children), by all means do it. You will earn brownie points with everyone, perhaps even including your former spouse.

Here's an example. A man with two children agreed to pay $1,200 a month in child support after the divorce. As time went along, he also picked up the cost of music lessons and tuition to a music camp for his kids, along with other costs he was not obligated to pay.

When the man asked to extend his weekend visitation by allowing the children to sleep over on Sunday, the mother of the children refused.

Under the law, child support itself is not tied to visitation. But in court, the man's generosity was a central theme. Besides providing more money, he had consented when his ex-wife asked to use *his* lake house for a family reunion. And he had stood by when she had a surgical procedure and needed extended help with the kids.

The point is that people who act in a reasonable, responsible manner get special consideration in most family courts. Over the objection of the woman, the man was granted his extra night of visitation.

In my experience with the family courts, reason and generosity trump indiscriminate toughness any day, giving you an extra card to play when necessary. It will make your children respect you more, and may even make your ex easier to deal with over the long haul.

Contempt Actions

Sometimes generosity is taken as weakness, reason as waffling by the opposition in a divorce. In those cases, enforcing a court order can be the most trying part of the divorce process.

When one party to a divorce simply won't comply with the law, an action for contempt against the offending party may be necessary. Contempt is used to enforce the payment of child support, certain types of financial and property matters and attorney's fees, or child custody and visitation orders. The standard for contempt is fairly understandable. One party must willfully refuse to comply with a specific order of the court that is central to the obligation in question. For example, if your ex has failed to pay child support, even though he has worked during the entire time of the contemptuous behavior and has chosen to spend the money on other things, most likely he is in contempt of court.

It's a different case if the opposing party has lost a job through no fault of his own, did not have an income during the time that child support payments went unpaid, did not have any assets to sell to satisfy the child support obligation and has no other means to pay the support or borrow money to pay it. Resolution of this issue will depend on the circumstances surrounding the failure to comply with the decree and the party's ability to explain the job loss. Likewise, a parent can be held in contempt for failing to comply with a visitation schedule or for not returning the child to the custodial parent after a visitation.

In a contempt action, you are asking the court to put the opposing party in jail or pay a fine for his or her failure to comply with the decree. Sometimes this drastic action is necessary to show the offending party that the obligation must be met; that what the judge ordered isn't just a mere *suggestion* of the action you should take.

Jail time is serious stuff, and you must ask yourself if you really want to put your children's mother or father in the slammer? You must weigh the seriousness of the contempt against the stark reality of jailing your ex-mate.

Under a contempt action, a party may be placed in jail for the contempt and released by purging the contempt action. For example, the court may order the party to jail until all or most of the back child support is paid. If the party is financially unable to pay, the court may not keep that person in jail. But in many cases, relatives or new spouses come forward to pay the amount due. It is amazing how quickly a person can cough up the cash when nonpayment means going to jail.

You can often predict compliance problems with your former spouse well before the final resolution of the case. Sometimes people make threats to withhold child support. These threats should be taken seriously, but don't overreact until it actually happens. If the party begins acting contemptuously, you need to keep detailed records of obligations that have not been met.

Standing Up to Your Ex

Before filing a contempt action, you need to give your ex adequate time to comply. But it's important not to wait too long to file. Many clients wait until they are owed tens of thousands of dollars or a visitation problem has festered into a real difficulty before filing an action. Even if a contempt action for missed child support payments is successful, you may have to accept installment payments to enable the opposing party to pay off the large debt. Each party should keep detailed records of support payments received or paid under the divorce decree, just in case a contempt action becomes necessary.

A contempt action needs to be filed soon after the party fails to comply so the offending party realizes you will punish noncompliance. Your relationship with the opposing party will be directly related to your initial actions after the divorce. You need to establish that you will not tolerate missed child support payments or your ex refusing to return the child at a scheduled time. Most likely, you will open yourself to charges that you are inflexible. But by establishing precedents, you may be able to limit future contemptuous behavior.

Former spouses who constantly refuse to abide by the decree should be placed in jail. This is an unfortunate situation. But when the sheriff takes one party to jail for contempt, great efforts are made to work out problems in a hurry.

CHAPTER TWENTY-FIVE

When All Else Fails, Modify

Most divorces are concluded within a few months. Others linger because of motions for a new trial or appeals. A few go on for years, due to efforts to modify the divorce decree.

The most common modifications involve child custody, child support and visitation. No party to a divorce should say at the outset that what happens in the original divorce action isn't important because a modification can be obtained. Modifications are expensive and disruptive to the lives of everyone involved. You should think long and hard about the effect of any return to the court system. Is this action entirely necessary? Are there other ways to accomplish what you want? And will the positive effect of the modification offset the negative effect of bringing the action?

The requirement for almost any modification is that a "material change of circumstance" has taken place since the last court hearing. This means there is a basic change in the lives of the parents or the children, which makes a modification of the terms of the divorce desirable.

A Change of Custody

As noted before, joint custody is the preferred arrangement in most Texas courts. But joint custody doesn't mean equal parenting, and so conflicts arise because of misunderstandings about the statutory role of parents. Sometimes these conflicts become so severe that one parent attempts to modify child custody or the terms of a joint custody arrangement. This is the most drastic and difficult form of modification to a divorce decree.

The parent asking for modification of the terms and conditions of the joint custody arrangement must show a material change of circumstance or that the order has become unworkable or inappropriate *and* that changing the custody arrangement will be a positive improvement for the child. The exact burden in these situations depends on the circumstances of the custody arrangement in place.

When a modification is contemplated, lines are drawn. Friends and family members take sides, many to testify if the action gets to court. Often, one parent will bring a custody modification when the actual conflict is between the parents and really there is no impact on the child except for the fighting.

What you, as a parent, must decide is whether the child has been harmed or *you* are upset. If your ex remarries or has a new relationship, this does not mean the child's situation always changes for the worse. I've seen parents demonize the ex's new partner so badly in the child's mind that the child feels he or she is being harmed. In cases like this, attempts to restrict the remarrying parent's access to the child can backfire on the parent who is obviously seeking revenge.

But what if the parent and his or her new partner engage in

sexual conduct in front of the child? What if there are provable signs of physical abuse, drug abuse or other criminal conduct, undue mental pressure on the child or neglect? What if there are no outward signs of abuse, but one parent is often intoxicated and endangers the child by driving drunk with that child in the car?

The judge or jury wants to know what is in the best interest of the *child*, not the parents. In determining whether to modify custody or change the conservator the child lives with on a primary basis, the court looks at a number of factors, including:

- The overall performance of the child in the home of the current primary conservator, including grades in school, general health, etc.;
- Desires of the child (the importance of this depends on the age and maturity level of the child);
- Activities and friends of the child;
- Stability of the respective parents and their home life;
- Ability of the parents to provide for the child both in economic resources and time; and
- Parents' travel schedules.

If one parent who has the child during the week is unable to get the child at school on time, it makes sense to determine if the other parent is better able to perform that function. If the custodial parent avoids living near families with children and the other parent loves to have kids in the house, maybe some alteration in custody is warranted.

Under Texas law, it can't be a matter of which parent offers the most economic resources. Without examining the specifics of two households, state law doesn't dictate that living in a million-dollar mansion is better for a child than being raised in a mobile home.

Custody cases usually begin with the social workers employed by the court system. Most urban counties have at least one counselor who studies the parties and their households in these cases to determine their fitness, and reports their findings to the court.

Most cases — including modifications — are scheduled for mediation, and a great number are settled out of court. Settlements take place when you get what you want or when you realize that you can't accomplish everything you would like. Because changes of custody are so difficult, many people are upset to find that they may not be able to change the conditions in which their children are living. That is why it's so important to pursue The Successful Divorce under your original decree.

Sometimes, one parent is not ready to assume the primary conservator role or doesn't feel he or she will be awarded this role in the divorce. Already, we've talked about parents who asked for joint custody, with an eye to seeing how the ex handles the single parent role. Patience is essential in these matters, and some parents wait to try for sole custody in a year or two.

Joint custody and the mediation system have cut down on the number of full-blown custody trials, but they still take place when an intractable issue is confronted or one parent or the other decides to play hardball with the system. Sometimes the way you approached the original trial affects the outcome of the trial for modification. It is shocking how many parents agree to give an abusive parent either joint custody or substantial visitation rights with a child that parent has abused during the marriage. It is difficult to convince a trial judge during a modification proceeding that the other parent's access should be limited when you've granted that parent expanded visitation even though you know that abuse occurred.

Evidence presented in a motion to modify custody must concern matters that occured *since* the decree or the last order of the court in this case. The trial judge will not allow the parties to dredge up complaints that should have been considered when the prior order was signed. Only in narrow circumstances, such as showing a continuing course of conduct, will this be allowed.

Custody trials are street battles that divide entire families and sets of friends. They cost enormous amounts of money in fees for attorneys and expert witnesses. They involve the lives of parents, children, friends and associates being examined as to their suitability as parents and people. Family law certainly involves more emotion and tension than any other area of the law, and the trial to modify custody is one of the most tension-filled and emotional actions of all.

But "winning" a modification of child custody can be the most rewarding of all parental actions, if your child's quality of life is at stake. Before you decide to take such a course, you should think about the following:

- How will this action affect my child?
- How will it affect me and other family members?
- Can I count on friends and family members to help me with this, including testifying in court if necessary?
- Am I prepared to invest the time and money to accomplish this?
- Can I afford it?
- What is the best outcome I can reasonably expect and

what's the downside of taking action?

- What will happen if I don't pursue this action?

These are questions you and your attorney should discuss before making a decision to seek a change in custody.

More or Less Child Support

A financial windfall for either party to a divorce, after the divorce is over, should benefit the children just as it would if the family had remained intact. Kids get new bicycles and larger rooms in fancier houses when the parents make more money. Increases or decreases in the income of either party influence modifications to prior child support awards.

If the obligor spouse's income has increased significantly, the custodial parent may be entitled to more child support. If the obligor spouse has lost a job or decreased his income significantly, the amount of child support he pays may be reduced. Periodic changes in the child support guidelines may be reason enough for payments to increase.

Both parents have a duty to support their children as best they can. What do you do, however, if the parent making child support payments pays for expenses and activities over and above the mandated child support obligation? You may not want to risk having those extra payments discontinued by fighting for a slight increase in child support. Most divorce experts can calculate the projected new child support payment under your facts, provided you have the gross monthly income figures for both parents as well as any day care and health insurance expenses.

Sometimes obligor parents take defensive actions when called on to pay more child support. An example: a noncustodial parent may attempt to seek custody when the child support modification action is filed. This action may be apparent to the court as an effort to avoid paying higher child support, but it can create considerable problems and expense for the custodial parent who is seeking an increase in child support.

If you have had less than exemplary conduct since the divorce, you may not want to ask for a modification of child support because custody could come into question. The fact that you, as a custodial parent, are living with a friend of the opposite sex may not seem like a big deal to you. But it can cloud the issue of child support and lead to a counter-petition by the other parent for custody of the children.

For every action in family court, there is an equal and opposite reaction. Modifications give rise to many reactions that people may have never considered in advance.

Access to Both Parents

The preference in the courts and in society is for good parents to have as much access to their children as possible. After the heat of divorce has cooled, many parents control kids' schedules between themselves. Informal modifications are common, but they aren't enforceable by law. Most parents find that as their children get older, they all need a little flexibility. This cooperation is recommended, as long as you feel comfortable with the changes and the fact that they are not mandated by the courts.

Quite often, those changes involve a noncustodial parent being granted more time with the children. A teenage child may want to take a long trip with that parent or spend an entire summer with the noncustodial grandparents. Some changes are brought about by refinements in the visitation guidelines. For instance, some parents who would otherwise take the children home on a Sunday night after a weekend visitation now keep the children Sunday night and take them to school the next morning. Each request should be carefully considered by the custodial parent, keeping in mind the needs of the child, the ability of the other parent to accept this responsibility and how the changes may affect your future rights.

The noncustodial parent should not begin to believe that each time such a request is made, the other parent *has* to go along with it. The other parent has rights and does not have to grant any variations to the agreed-upon visitation schedule.

Visitation changes are often mediated by the social workers in family court services, after interviewing parents and sometimes seeking information from friends and family members.

These modifications, like all others, are expensive to achieve if you have to go to court. You might spend several thousand dollars to get one additional evening of visitation or to deny your ex that amount of time with your children. Remember, your children invariably get older and circumstances change. If you and your ex-spouse can remain flexible and reasonable, you can avoid a lot of heartache down the road.

Changes That Aren't Called Modifications

Occasionally, one party to a divorce has been known to hide a piece of property so that it will not become part of the divorce settlement. In cases like this, if the other party is able to locate the property, he or she can petition the court to reopen the case and take the found property into consideration in the total settlement.

If a certain kind of fraud takes place during the pendency of the divorce and is not discovered until after the divorce is final, the trial court judge can set aside the division of property. How long you have to bring such a cause of action can vary depending on the facts of the case. A bill of review is a proceeding that seeks to set aside the division of property. These are complicated procedures that your attorney can detail for you if you feel something went wrong in this area.

CHAPTER TWENTY-SIX

The Successful Divorce

You are a bundle of conflicting emotions. You are hurt and angry, confused and stunned. You are certain no one has ever felt this bad. You look back on the painful memories of a loveless marriage and ahead to a worse future. You think of yourself as powerless, friendless, without joy. You are facing divorce, and divorce is just no fun — not for you, your children, your family or your friends. Even though you might not believe it now, it's no fun for your soon-to-be ex and those around that person, no matter who decided this divorce was necessary.

At precisely this moment, when you feel the worst, you must decide what kind of divorce you will have. You can remain a victim, allowing yourself to be pushed around. You can decide to become a vindictive person, extracting your vengeance on everyone involved. Or you can decide that this will be a different kind of divorce. That the kids can be kids, without having to take on unnecessary baggage. And the older people will act like adults, instead of portraying adolescents. Out of all this can come a brighter future, people with greater stability and maturity. You can emerge financially and emotionally intact.

Successful Divorce Principles

If you dedicate yourself to achieving The Successful Divorce, the following principles will help you:

- Decide if divorce really is the answer for you.
- Look for resolution, not revenge.
- Don't confuse what's best for the children with what satisfies your vengeful side.
- Hire the most experienced family law attorney you can afford and one who matches your personality.
- Try to keep your divorce uncontested.
- Mediate in good faith.
- Stockpile useful family information.
- Be truthful with your attorney.
- Decide who gets which assets between you and your spouse. Don't let a judge or jury decide for you, if possible.
- Decide what's in the best interest of your children and follow that path.
- Don't be too greedy.
- If your spouse concedes something he or she doesn't have to, be grateful.
- If mediation fails, get ready for trial.
- Present yourself well before the judge or jury.
- Remember that if you don't get everything you want, your life is not over.

- Consider this: Will this divorce settlement leave me and my family in a good situation, whether I remarry or not.

Divorce is a mixed bag of complex issues. You have to look at the way your life is today, tomorrow and into the future. The settlement agreement needs to address every possible issue you can imagine that may arise after divorce, because it is extremely difficult and expensive to modify a divorce agreement. Remember that if you and your spouse have not been able to agree *during* the marriage, you probably will not be able to agree on very much *after* the marriage.

When you are in the midst of a divorce, the last thing you want to consider is getting married again. But statistics tell us that well over half the people who get divorced for the first time will remarry. Your chances for happiness are narrowed considerably if you leave yourself financially wounded and with a difficult custody arrangement. Bad divorces can make remarriage too costly and a full life nearly impossible.

I knew about a young man who gave his wife custody of their children and all the marital assets. And he was paying exorbitant child support after a divorce that was not his idea. He did it, he said, "because I didn't want my kids to suffer." When questioned about the competence of his attorney, the man said, "I gave my ex-wife all of that, and I didn't think I needed an attorney." Three months after the divorce was final, she moved 2,000 miles away to live with a man they had both considered a friend. The young ex-husband is alone now, with no money and significant debt. He makes the trip once a year to see his children and his assets. And even if he wanted to remarry, he feels unable to handle the emotional and financial obligations involved in taking on a new relationship.

An Attorney Can Represent Only One Party

The only way to avoid such a tragedy is to consult with an expert in matrimonial law in your area before proceeding with a divorce action. Do not execute any documents without the advice and approval of an attorney. Furthermore, do not rely on the advice of your spouse's attorney in making a determination of what is an appropriate settlement. Your spouse's attorney cannot advise you as to the consequences of your actions; his sole purpose is to protect your spouse.

Regrettably, everyone you talk to is a specialist in divorce, including your hair stylist or grocery clerk. Each of these people has a cousin who got a divorce somewhere, and you need to do what they did. You will be advised by everyone you meet. My suggestion is to listen and be polite, then consult with someone who knows Texas law.

It is likely that your divorce will be one of the most difficult issues you will have to deal with during your lifetime. Do not believe that your spouse will do "what's right" and nothing will go wrong. Consult with an attorney about the actions needed to protect yourself, and get prepared to go into battle. Hopefully, you will avoid going to war. But if you are prepared to do so, you will likely prevent a bad situation from becoming an impossible one.

The Successful Divorce Is Now

It's like a woman seeking to modify her divorce decree told her attorney: "I had no idea how much of my future would be closely related to the divorce agreement I signed years ago. If only I had been aware of all the issues that would come up and would have hired an expert at that time."

Now she understands what's necessary to obtain The Successful Divorce.

Resources

Texas Attorney General's Office
800/252-8014 automated line
512/460-6000 for office nearest you

State Bar of Texas
800/204-2222

Child Protective Services
800/252-5400 to report child abuse

Texas Fathers for Equal Rights

Dallas	214/741-4800	Odessa	915/362-5624
Fort Worth	817/457-3237	Paris	214/785-9365

ACES
(Asso. for Children for Enforcement of Support)   214/553-5935

Divorce Recovery Classes

Family Support Services (Amarillo)	806/372-3202
109th Judicial District (Andrews)	915/524-1429
Family Services of Beaumont	409/833-2668
Central Texas MHMR (Brownwood)	915/646-9574
Family Counseling (Corpus Christi)	
EXCAP (Dallas)	972/644-2098
YWCA El Paso	915/577-9922
Kids First (Fort Worth)	817/923-3348
Children Cope (Houston)	713/952-2673
Centers for Children and Families (Midland)	915/570-1084
Family Service Ctr of Port Arthur	409/983-4591
Family Serv. Asso. of San Antonio	210/340-1818
Red River Clinic (Sherman)	903/892-0931
Family Counseling/Children's Serv.	254/751-1777

Grandparents Raising Grandchildren
817/577-0435

References

1. Bureau of Vital Statistics, 1995-96. Monthly Vital Statistics Report, Vol. 45, No.12. (July 17, 1997).

2. *Texas Almanac* (Dallas: The Dallas Morning News, Inc., 1996).

3. Walker, Rob. "T&C's Guide to Civilized Divorce," "America's Top Divorce Lawyers." *Town & Country* (January 1998): 119-121.

4. State Bar of Texas, Austin. Telephone inquiry (June 18, 1998).

5. Kristof, Kathy. Personal Finance column. Business section, *The Dallas Morning News.* (Los Angeles Times Syndicate, October 26, 1997): 5H.

6. Ibid.

7. Tannen, Deborah. *The Argument Culture: Moving From Debate to Dialogue* (New York: Random House, 1998).

8. National Coalition Against Domestic Violence statistics, 1996.

9. Bradburn-Stern, Bev. "Is Getting A Divorce Too Easy?" *Children Cope With Divorce Newsletter* (Summer 1997).

10. Texas Family Code, State of Texas, Parent-Child Relationship, 154.126, 1998. Guidelines were added by Acts 1995, 74th Leg., Ch. 20, Section 1, effective April 20, 1995.

11. Ussery, Lynn. ACES (Association for Children for Enforcement of Support). Telephone inquiry, July 1998.

12. Lake, Steven R. and Feldman, Ruth Duskin. *Rematch* (Chicago: Chicago Review Press, 1989).

13. Legal Information Network. Parsons Technology, 1998.

14. Lake and Feldman.

15. Upshaw, Larry. "The Age of Divorce." *D Magazine* (May 1995): 65-72.

Standard Possession Order

The Court finds that the following provisions of this Standard Possession Order are intended to and do comply with the requirements of Texas Family Code sections 153.311 through 153.317. IT IS ORDERED that Sole Managing Conservator and Possessory Conservator shall comply with all terms and conditions of this Standard Possession Order. IT IS ORDERED that this Standard Possession Order is effective immediately and applies to all periods of possession occurring on and after the signing of this Standard Possession Order. IT IS, THEREFORE, ORDERED:

(a) Definitions

1. In this Standard Possession Order "school" means the primary or secondary school in which the child is enrolled or, if the child is not enrolled in a primary or secondary school, the public school district in which the child primarily resides.

2. In this Standard Possession Order "child" includes each child, whether one or more, who is a subject of this suit while that child is under the age of eighteen years and not otherwise emancipated.

(b) Mutual Agreement or Specified Terms for Possession

IT IS ORDERED that the conservators shall have possession of the child at times mutually agreed to in advance by the parties, and, in the absence of mutual agreement, it is ORDERED that the conservators shall have possession of the child under the specified terms set out in this Standard Possession Order.

(c) Parents Who Reside 100 Miles or Less Apart

Except as otherwise explicitly provided in this Standard Possession Order, when Possessory Conservator resides 100 miles or less from the primary residence of the child, Possessory Conservator shall have the right to possession of the child as follows:

1. Weekends — On weekends, beginning at [select one: 6:00 p.m./the time the child's school is regularly dismissed/or specify other time elected between school dismissal and 6:00 p.m.], on the first, third, and fifth Friday of each month and ending at [select one: 6:00 p.m. on the following Sunday/the time the child's school resumes after the weekend].

2. Weekend Possession Extended by a Holiday — Except as otherwise explicitly provided in this Standard Possession Order, if a weekend period of possession by Possessory Conservator begins on a Friday that is a school holiday during the regular school term or a federal, state, or local holiday during the summer months when school is not in session, or if the period ends on or is immediately followed by a Monday that is such a holiday, that weekend period of possession shall begin at [select one: 6:00 p.m./the time the child's school is regularly dismissed/or specify other time elected between school dismissal and 6:00 p.m.] on the Thursday immediately preceding the Friday holiday or school holiday or end [select one: at 6:00 p.m. on that Monday holiday or school holiday/at 6:00 p.m. on that Monday

holiday or at the time school resumes after that school holiday], as applicable.

3.   Wednesdays — On Wednesday of each week during the regular school term, beginning at [select one: 6:00 p.m./the time the child's school is regularly dismissed/or specify other time elected between school dismissal and 6:00 p.m.] and ending at [select one: 8:00 p.m./the time the child's school resumes on Thursday].

4.   Christmas Holidays in Even-Numbered Years — In even-numbered years, beginning at [select one: 6:00 p.m./the time the child's school is regularly dismissed/or specify other time elected between school dismissal and 6:00 p.m.] on the day the child is dismissed from school for the Christmas school vacation and ending at noon on December 26.

5.   Christmas Holidays in Odd-Numbered Years — In odd-numbered years, beginning at noon on December 26 and ending at [select one: 6:00 p.m. on the day before/the time] the child's school resumes after that Christmas school vacation.

6.   Thanksgiving in Odd-Numbered Years — In odd-numbered years, beginning at [select one: 6:00 p.m./the time the child's school is regularly dismissed/or specify other time elected between school dismissal and 6:00 p.m.] on the day the child is dismissed from school for the Thanksgiving holiday and ending at [select one: 6:00 p.m. on the Sunday following Thanksgiving/the time the child's school resumes after that Thanksgiving holiday].

7.   Spring Break in Even-Numbered Years — In even-num-

bered years, beginning at [select one: 6:00 p.m./the time the child's school is regularly dismissed/or specify other time elected between school dismissal and 6:00 p.m.] on the day the child is dismissed from school for the school's spring vacation and ending at [select one: 6:00 p.m. on the day before/the time] school resumes after that vacation.

8. Extended Summer Possession by Possessory Conservator

With Written Notice by May 1— If Possessory Conservator gives Sole Managing Conservator written notice by May 1 of a year specifying an extended period or periods of summer possession for that year, Possessory Conservator shall have possession of the child for thirty days beginning no earlier than the day after the child's school is dismissed for the summer vacation and ending no later than seven days before school resumes at the end of the summer vacation in that year, to be exercised in no more than two separate periods of at least seven consecutive days each, as specified in the written notice. These periods of possession shall begin and end at 6:00 p.m.

Without Written Notice by May 1— If Possessory Conservator does not give Sole Managing Conservator written notice by May 1 of a year specifying an extended period or periods of summer possession for that year, Possessory Conservator shall have possession of the child for thirty consecutive days in that year beginning at 6:00 p.m. on July 1 and ending at 6:00 p.m. on July 31.

9. Child's Birthday — If Possessory Conservator is not otherwise entitled under this Standard Possession Order to present pos-

session of the child on the child's birthday, Possessory Conservator shall have possession of the child [include if desired: and the child's siblings] beginning at 6:00 p.m. and ending at 8:00 p.m. on that day, provided that Possessory Conservator picks up the child from Sole Managing Conservator's residence and returns the child to that same place.

10. Father's Day Weekend — Each year, beginning at 6:00 p.m. on the Friday preceding Father's Day and ending at 6:00 p.m. on Father's Day, provided that if he is not otherwise entitled under this Standard Possession Order to present possession of the child, he shall pick up the child from Sole Managing Conservator's residence and return the child to that same place.

11. Mother's Day Weekend — Each year, beginning at 6:00 p.m. on the Friday preceding Mother's Day and ending at 6:00 p.m. on Mother's Day, provided that if she is not otherwise entitled under this Standard Possession Order to present possession of the child, she shall pick up the child from Sole Managing Conservator's residence and return the child to that same place.

Notwithstanding the weekend and Wednesday periods of possession ORDERED for Possessory Conservator, it is explicitly ORDERED that Sole Managing Conservator shall have a superior right of possession of the child as follows:

1. Christmas Holidays in Odd-Numbered Years — In odd-numbered years, beginning at 6:00 p.m. on the day the child is dismissed from school for the Christmas school vacation and ending at

noon on December 26.

2. Christmas Holidays in Even-Numbered Years — In even-numbered years, beginning at noon on December 26 and ending at 6:00 p.m. on the day before school resumes after that Christmas school vacation.

3. Thanksgiving in Even-Numbered Years — In even-numbered years, beginning at 6:00 p.m. on the day the child is dismissed from school for the Thanksgiving holiday and ending at 6:00 p.m. on the following Sunday.

4. Spring Break in Odd-Numbered Years — In odd-numbered years, beginning at 6:00 p.m. on the day the child is dismissed from school for the school's spring vacation and ending at 6:00 p.m. on the day before school resumes after that vacation.

5. Summer Weekend Possession by Sole Managing Conservator — If Sole Managing Conservator gives Possessory Conservator written notice by June 1 of a year, Sole Managing Conservator shall have possession of the child on any one weekend beginning at 6:00 p.m. on Friday and ending at 6:00 p.m. on the following Sunday during any one period of the extended summer possession by Possessory Conservator in that year, provided that Sole Managing Conservator picks up the child from Possessory Conservator and returns the child to that same place.

6. Extended Summer Possession by Sole Managing Conservator — If Sole Managing Conservator gives Possessory Conservator

written notice by May 15 of a year or gives Possessory Conservator fourteen days' written notice on or after May 16 of a year, Sole Managing Conservator may designate one weekend beginning no earlier than the day after the child's school is dismissed for the summer vacation and ending no later than seven days before school resumes at the end of the summer vacation, during which an otherwise scheduled weekend period of possession by Possessory Conservator shall not take place in that year, provided that the weekend so designated does not interfere with Possessory Conservator's period or periods of extended summer possession [include if applicable: or with Father's Day Weekend].

7.   Child's Birthday — If Sole Managing Conservator is not otherwise entitled under this Standard Possession Order to present possession of the child on the child's birthday, Sole Managing Conservator shall have possession of the child [include if desired: and the child's siblings] beginning at 6:00 p.m. and ending at 8:00 p.m. on that day, provided that Sole Managing Conservator picks up the child from Possessory Conservator's residence and returns the child to that same place.

8.   Father's Day Weekend — Each year, beginning at 6:00 p.m. on the Friday preceding Father's Day and ending at 6:00 p.m. on Father's Day, provided that if Sole Managing Conservator is not otherwise entitled under this Standard Possession Order to present possession of the child, he shall pick up the child from Possessory Conservator's residence and return the child to that same place.

8.   Mother's Day Weekend — Each year, beginning at 6:00 p.m.

on the Friday preceding Mother's Day and ending at 6:00 p.m. on Mother's Day, provided that if Sole Managing Conservator is not otherwise entitled under this Standard Possession Order to present possession of the child, she shall pick up the child from Possessory Conservator's residence and return the child to that same place.

Sole Managing Conservator shall have the right of possession of the child at all other times not specifically designated in this Standard Possession Order for Possessory Conservator.

(d) Parents Who Reside More Than 100 Miles Apart

Except as otherwise explicitly provided in this Standard Possession Order, when Possessory Conservator resides more than 100 miles from the residence of the child, Possessory Conservator shall have the right to possession of the child as follows:

1. Weekends — Unless Possessory Conservator elects the alternative period of weekend possession described in the next paragraph, Possessory Conservator shall have the right to possession of the child on weekends, beginning at [select one: 6:00 p.m./the time the child's school is regularly dismissed/or specify other time elected between school dismissal and 6:00 p.m.], on the first, third, and fifth Friday of each month and ending at [select one: 6:00 p.m. on the following Sunday/the time the child's school resumes after the weekend]. Except as otherwise explicitly provided in this Standard Possession Order, if such a weekend period of possession by Possessory Conservator begins on a Friday that is a school holiday during the regular school term or a federal, state, or local holiday during the summer

months when school is not in session, or if the period ends on or is immediately followed by a Monday that is such a holiday, that weekend period of possession shall begin at [select one: 6:00 p.m./the time the child's school is regularly dismissed/or specify other time elected between school dismissal and 6:00 p.m.] on the Thursday immediately preceding the Friday holiday or school holiday or end [select one: at 6:00 p.m. on that Monday holiday or school holiday/ at 6:00 p.m. on that Monday holiday or at the time school resumes after that school holiday], as applicable.

Alternate weekend possession — In lieu of the weekend possession described in the foregoing paragraph, Possessory Conservator shall have the right to possession of the child not more than one weekend per month of Possessory Conservator's choice beginning at [select one: 6:00 p.m./the time the child's school is regularly dismissed/or specify other time elected between school dismissal and 6:00 p.m.] on the day school recesses for the weekend and ending at [select one: 6:00 p.m. on the day before school resumes/the time the child's school resumes] after the weekend. Except as otherwise explicitly provided in this Standard Possession Order, if such a weekend period of possession by Possessory Conservator begins on a Friday that is a school holiday during the regular school term or a federal, state, or local holiday during the summer months when school is not in session, or if the period ends on or is immediately followed by a Monday that is such a holiday, that weekend period of possession shall begin at [select one: 6:00 p.m./the time the child's school is regularly dismissed/or specify other time elected between school dismissal and 6:00 p.m.] on the Thursday immediately preceding the Friday holiday or school holiday or end [select one: at 6:00 p.m.

on that Monday holiday or school holiday/at 6:00 p.m. on that Monday holiday or at the time school resumes after that school holiday], as applicable. Possessory Conservator may elect an option for this alternative period of weekend possession by giving written notice to Sole Managing Conservator within ninety days after the parties begin to reside more than 100 miles apart. If Possessory Conservator makes this election, Possessory Conservator shall give Managing Conservator fourteen days' written or telephonic notice preceding a designated weekend. The weekends chosen shall not conflict with the provisions regarding Christmas, Thanksgiving, the child's birthday, and [Father's/Mother's] Day Weekend below.

1. Weekends — On weekends, beginning at [select one: 6:00 p.m./the time the child's school is regularly dismissed/or specify other time elected between school dismissal and 6:00 p.m.] on the first, third, and fifth Friday of each month, and ending at [select one: 6:00 p.m. on the following Sunday/the time the child's school resumes after the weekend]. Except as otherwise explicitly provided in this Standard Possession Order, if a weekend period of possession by Possessory Conservator begins on a Friday that is a school holiday during the regular school term or a federal, state, or local holiday during the summer months when school is not in session, or if the period ends on or is immediately followed by a Monday that is such a holiday, that weekend period of possession shall begin at [select one: 6:00 p.m./the time the child's school is regularly dismissed/or specify other time elected between school dismissal and 6:00 p.m.] on the Thursday immediately preceding the Friday holiday or school holiday or end [select one: at 6:00 p.m. on that Monday holiday or school holiday/at 6:00 p.m. on that Monday holiday or at the time

school resumes after that school holiday], as applicable.

1.   Weekend — One weekend per month, of Possessory Conservator's choice, beginning at [select one: 6:00 p.m./the time the child's school is regularly dismissed/or specify other time elected between school dismissal and 6:00 p.m.] on the day school recesses for the weekend and ending at [select one: 6:00 p.m. on the day before school resumes/the time the child's school resumes] after the weekend, provided that Possessory Conservator gives Sole Managing Conservator fourteen days' written or telephonic notice preceding a designated weekend. The weekends chosen shall not conflict with the provisions regarding Christmas, Thanksgiving, the child's birthday, and [Father's/Mother's] Day Weekend below.

2.   Christmas Holidays in Even-Numbered Years — In even-numbered years, beginning at [select one: 6:00 p.m./the time the child's school is regularly dismissed/or specify other time elected between school dismissal and 6:00 p.m.] on the day the child is dismissed from school for the Christmas school vacation and ending at noon on December 26.

3.   Christmas Holidays in Odd-Numbered Years — In odd-numbered years, beginning at noon on December 26 and ending at [select one: 6:00 p.m. on the day before/the time] the child's school resumes after that Christmas school vacation.

4.   Thanksgiving in Odd-Numbered Years — In odd-numbered years, beginning at [select one: 6:00 p.m./the time the child's school is regularly dismissed/or specify other time elected between school

dismissal and 6:00 p.m.] on the day the child is dismissed from school for the Thanksgiving holiday and ending at [select one: 6:00 p.m. on the Sunday following Thanksgiving/the time the child's school resumes after that Thanksgiving holiday].

5. Spring Break in All Years — Every year, beginning at [select one: 6:00 p.m./the time the child's school is regularly dismissed/or specify other time elected between school dismissal and 6:00 p.m.] on the day the child is dismissed from school for the school's spring vacation and ending at [select one: 6:00 p.m. on the day before/the time] school resumes after that vacation.

6. Extended Summer Possession by Possessory Conservator —

With Written Notice by May 1 — If Possessory Conservator gives Sole Managing Conservator written notice by May 1 of a year specifying an extended period or periods of summer possession for that year, Possessory Conservator shall have possession of the child for forty-two days beginning no earlier than the day after the child's school is dismissed for the summer vacation and ending no later than seven days before school resumes at the end of the summer vacation in that year, to be exercised in no more than two separate periods of at least seven consecutive days each, as specified in the written notice. These periods of possession shall begin and end at 6:00 p.m.

Without Written Notice by May 1 — If Possessory Conservator does not give Sole Managing Conservator written notice by May 1 of a year specifying an extended period or periods of summer possession for that year, Possessory Conservator shall have possession of the child for forty-two consecutive days beginning at 6:00 p.m. on June 15 and ending at 6:00 p.m. on July 27 of that year.

7. Child's Birthday — If Possessory Conservator is not otherwise entitled under this Standard Possession Order to present possession of the child on the child's birthday, Possessory Conservator shall have possession of the child [include if desired: and the child's siblings] beginning at 6:00 p.m. and ending at 8:00 p.m. on that day, provided that Possessory Conservator picks up the child from Sole Managing Conservator's residence and returns the child to that same place.

8. Father's Day Weekend — Each year, beginning at 6:00 p.m. on the Friday preceding Father's Day and ending at 6:00 p.m. on Father's Day, provided that if Possessory Conservator is not otherwise entitled under this Standard Possession Order to present possession of the child, he shall pick up the child from Sole Managing Conservator's residence and return the child to that same place.

8. Mother's Day Weekend — Each year, beginning at 6:00 p.m. on the Friday preceding Mother's Day and ending at 6:00 p.m. on Mother's Day, provided that if Possessory Conservator is not otherwise entitled under this Standard Possession Order to present possession of the child, she shall pick up the child from Sole Managing Conservator's residence and return the child to that same place.

Notwithstanding the weekend periods of possession ORDERED for Possessory Conservator, it is explicitly ORDERED that Sole Managing Conservator shall have a superior right of possession of the child as follows:

1.   Christmas Holidays in Odd-Numbered Years — In odd-numbered years, beginning at 6:00 p.m. on the day the child is dismissed from school for the Christmas school vacation and ending at noon on December 26.

2.   Christmas Holidays in Even-Numbered Years — In even-numbered years, beginning at noon on December 26 and ending at 6:00 p.m. on the day before school resumes after that Christmas school vacation.

3.   Thanksgiving in Even-Numbered Years — In even-numbered years, beginning at 6:00 p.m. on the day the child is dismissed from school for the Thanksgiving holiday and ending at 6:00 p.m. on the following Sunday.

4. Summer Weekend Possession by Sole Managing Conservator — If Sole Managing Conservator gives Possessory Conservator written notice by June 1 of a year, Sole Managing Conservator shall have possession of the child on any one weekend beginning at 6:00 p.m. on Friday and ending at 6:00 p.m. on the following Sunday during any one period of possession by Possessory Conservator during Possessory Conservator's extended summer possession in that year, provided that if a period of possession by Possessory Conservator in that year exceeds thirty days, Sole Managing Conservator may have possession of the child under the terms of this provision on any two nonconsecutive weekends during that period and provided that Sole

Managing Conservator picks up the child from Possessory Conservator and returns the child to that same place.

5. Extended Summer Possession by Sole Managing Conservator — If Sole Managing Conservator gives Possessory Conservator written notice by June 1 of a year, Sole Managing Conservator may designate twenty-one days beginning no earlier than the day after the child's school is dismissed for the summer vacation and ending no later than seven days before school resumes at the end of the summer vacation in that year, to be exercised in no more than two separate periods of at least seven consecutive days each, during which Possessory Conservator shall not have possession of the child, provided that the period or periods so designated do not interfere with Possessory Conservator's period or periods of extended summer possession [include if applicable: or with Father's Day Weekend].

6. Child's Birthday — If Sole Managing Conservator is not otherwise entitled under this Standard Possession Order to present possession of the child on the child's birthday, Sole Managing Conservator shall have possession of the child [include if desired: and the child's siblings] beginning at 6:00 p.m. and ending at 8:00 p.m. on that day, provided that Sole Managing Conservator picks up the child from Possessory Conservator's residence and returns the child to that same place.

7. Father's Day Weekend — Each year, beginning at 6:00 p.m. on the Friday preceding Father's Day and ending at 6:00 p.m. on Father's Day, provided that if Sole Managing Conservator is not otherwise entitled under this Standard Possession Order to present pos-

session of the child, he shall pick up the child from Possessory Conservator's residence and return the child to that same place.

7. Mother's Day Weekend — Each year, beginning at 6:00 p.m. on the Friday preceding Mother's Day and ending at 6:00 p.m. on Mother's Day, provided that if Sole Managing Conservator is not otherwise entitled under this Standard Possession Order to present possession of the child, she shall pick up the child from Possessory Conservator's residence and return the child to that same place.

Sole Managing Conservator shall have the right of possession of the child at all other times not specifically designated in this Standard Possession Order for Possessory Conservator.

(e) General Terms and Conditions

Except as otherwise explicitly provided in this Standard Possession Order, the terms and conditions of possession of the child that apply regardless of the distance between the residence of a parent and the child are as follows:

1. Surrender of Child by Sole Managing Conservator — Sole Managing Conservator is ORDERED to surrender the child to Possessory Conservator at the beginning of each period of Possessory Conservator's possession at the residence of Sole Managing Conservator.

If a period of possession by Possessory Conservator begins at the time the child's school is regularly dismissed, Sole Managing

Conservator is ORDERED to surrender the child to Possessory Conservator at the beginning of each such period of possession at the school in which the child is enrolled. If the child is not in school, Possessory Conservator shall pick up the child at the residence of Sole Managing Conservator at [time], and Sole Managing Conservator is ORDERED to surrender the child to Possessory Conservator at the residence of Sole Managing Conservator at [time] under these circumstances.

2. Surrender of Child by Possessory Conservator — Possessory Conservator is ORDERED to surrender the child to Sole Managing Conservator at the residence of Possessory Conservator at the end of each period of possession.

2. Return of Child by Possessory Conservator — Possessory Conservator is ORDERED to return the child to the residence of Sole Managing Conservator at the end of each period of possession. However, it is ORDERED that, if Sole Managing Conservator and Possessory Conservator live in the same county at the time of rendition of this order, Possessory Conservator's county of residence remains the same after rendition of this order, and Sole Managing Conservator's county of residence changes, effective on the date of the change of residence by Sole Managing Conservator, Possessory Conservator shall surrender the child to Sole Managing Conservator at the residence of Possessory Conservator at the end of each period of possession.

If a period of possession by Possessory Conservator ends at the time the child's school resumes, Possessory Conservator is ORDERED to surrender the child to Sole Managing Conservator at the end of each period of possession at the school in which the child is enrolled or, if the child is not in school, at the residence of Sole Managing Conservator at [time].

3. Surrender of Child by Possessory Conservator — Possessory Conservator is ORDERED to surrender the child to Sole Managing Conservator, if the child is in Possessory Conservator's possession or subject to Possessory Conservator's control, at the beginning of each period of Sole Managing Conservator's exclusive periods of possession, at the place designated in this Standard Possession Order.

4. Return of Child by Sole Managing Conservator — Sole Managing Conservator is
ORDERED to return the child to Possessory Conservator, if Possessory Conservator is entitled to possession of the child, at the end of each of Sole Managing exclusive periods of possession, at the place designated in this Standard Possession Order.

5. Personal Effects — Each conservator is ORDERED to return with the child the personal effects that the child brought at the beginning of the period of possession.

6. Designation of Competent Adult — Each conservator may designate any competent adult to pick up and return the child, as applicable. IT IS ORDERED that a conservator or a designated competent adult be present when the child is picked up or returned.

7. Inability to Exercise Possession — Each conservator is OR-DERED to give notice to the person in possession of the child on each occasion that the conservator will be unable to exercise that conservator's right of possession for any specified period.

8. Written Notice — Written notice shall be deemed to have been timely made if received or postmarked before or at the time that notice is due.

9. Notice to School and Sole Managing Conservator — If Possessory Conservator's time of possession of the child ends at the time school resumes and for any reason the child is not or will not be returned to school, Possessory Conservator shall immediately notify the school and Sole Managing Conservator that the child will not be or has not been returned to school.

This concludes the Standard Possession Order.

Notes:

Notes: